The Anatomy and Impact of

Cyberattacks

Published by
COPAL Publishing Group
E-143, Lajpat Nagar, Sahibabad
Distt. Ghaziabad, UP – 201005
INDIA
https://copalublishing.com

First Published 2025

ISBN: 978-81-974194-47

Printed and bound by D.K. Fine Art Press (P) Ltd.

The Anatomy and Impact of Cyberattacks

Asis Kumar Tripathy

COPAL PUBLISHING GROUP

Inspiring for a better future through publishing

Preface

Unseen Wars: The Anatomy and Impact of Cyber Attacks delves into the complex and evolving battlefield of cyberspace, where conflicts are waged silently yet leave profound global Implications. This book provides a comprehensive exploration of the anatomy, methods, and consequences of cyber-attacks, offering readers a detailed understanding of this often invisible but increasingly critical domain of modern warfare.

The volume is divided into key thematic sections:

- ***Anatomy of Cyber Attacks:*** Examining the techniques, tools, and strategies employed by hackers, state-sponsored actors, and other malicious entities.
- ***Case Studies:*** Analyzing real-world incidents that reveal the vulnerabilities in critical infrastructure, like, logo based phishing attack detection.
- ***Societal and Economic Impacts:*** Investigating the ripple effects of cyber attacks on global economies, geopolitics, and individual privacy.
- ***Defensive Strategies:*** Exploring the cutting-edge technologies and policies aimed at mitigating risks and enhancing resilience in the digital age.

Written by leading experts in cybersecurity, Unseen Wars combines scholarly insights with practical perspectives. It is an essential resource for industry leaders, cybersecurity professionals, and anyone interested in understanding how cyber threats are shaping the future of global security.

As cyber-attacks grow in scale and sophistication, this book equips readers with the knowledge needed to navigate the challenges of this shadowy yet omnipresent frontier.

Contents

1 Introduction

Abstract: Cyber warfare has emerged as a critical dimension of modern conflicts, targeting nations, organizations, and individuals with stealth and precision. Unlike conventional warfare, cyberattacks operate in the shadows, exploiting vulnerabilities in digital infrastructure to disrupt systems, steal sensitive data, and undermine national security. This chapter examines the anatomy of cyberattacks, including their tactics, techniques, and evolving methodologies. It also explores the broader impact of cyber warfare on economies, political stability, and global security. By analyzing real-world case studies, this study highlights the growing sophistication of cyber threats and the urgent need for robust cybersecurity measures to mitigate risks in an increasingly interconnected world.

Keywords: Cyber warfare, Digital threats, Cybersecurity, Hacking tactics, National security

1.1 Overview of Cyberattacks

Cyberattacks are malicious efforts aimed at violating the information systems that people and organizations use. Cyberattacks take various forms and may result in data theft, monetary loss, or even a loss of essential services. Cyberattacks have emerged as a significant threat, and recent trends show alarming rates of their occurrence. Malicious digital incursions exist in the categories of data breach, network infiltration, ransomware, and distributed denial-of-service attack. Cyberattacks have been proliferating in various forms and stages, resulting in enormous financial loss, compromise of sensitive data, and disruption of critical infrastructure on a global scale. One of the significant factors for increased cyberattacks is the explosive growth and quick adaptation of communication technologies and the widespread shift towards digital modes of operations across various industries and sectors. Such rapid digitalization has thrown a multitude of intricate vulnerabilities that an organization can't keep pace with the ever-changing and rapidly developing threat landscape. Cybercriminals now increasingly identify, exploit, and use these flaws in order to compromise critical infrastructures and data and the high-value asset that has highly destructive consequences through the loss of enormous amounts, disruption of the operation, as well as having breaches in personal data and sensitive data. As such, organizations need to emphasize implementing significant measures of cybersecurity that go beyond the assessment and continuous monitoring of risk and the adoption of advanced security technologies to mitigate the increased threats caused by cyberattacks. Furthermore, familiarity and comprehensive training programs for employees concerning cybersecurity will help strengthen a target organization's defenses from potential cyberattacks. The modern digital landscape has brought forth a very prevalent challenge: cyberattacks. These are indeed a changing threat—something that people, organizations, and governments around the world are now focused upon. Gradually, with each passing day, different kinds of cyberattacks are being documented, including but not limited to email bombing, data theft, denial-of-service attacks, Trojan attacks, and system hacking. These events are happening with increasing frequency, driven by the widespread growth of social media, increasing online activity, and growing time spent on digital platforms [1].

Cyber risk is one of the most increasing threats to public and private institutions alike, in that it threatens the disaster-like effects of organizational information systems damage, reputational damage, and a potential loss of consumer and stakeholder confidence. High levels of sophistication and frequency of cyberattacks can lead to heavy losses financially, disrupt operations significantly, and jeopardize sensitive data, thus undermining public trust and an institution's position in the community. Therefore, organizations must focus on implementing strong cybersecurity measures and employee training programs to mitigate these evolving threats and protect their digital assets. Cyberattacks are driven by a diverse mix of motives, which could be financial in nature, based on political or ideological goals, or driven by personal motivations. Many attackers target illegal gains from ransomware attacks, data theft, or extortions. Others carry out hacktivism, disrupting societal or political activities to raise the profile of such causes. Most state-sponsored attacks target critical infrastructure or sensitive information for espionage, sabotage, or strategic gain. While the reasons behind attackers vary from the satisfaction of creating chaos and revenge or even a personal vendetta, individuals and groups carrying out such detrimental activities are increasing in sophistication as cyberattack tools grow easier to obtain. The rapid spread of the COVID-19 pandemic has dramatically amplified the existing problem of cyberattacks as the forced move to remote work and further increased reliance on digital infrastructure has given

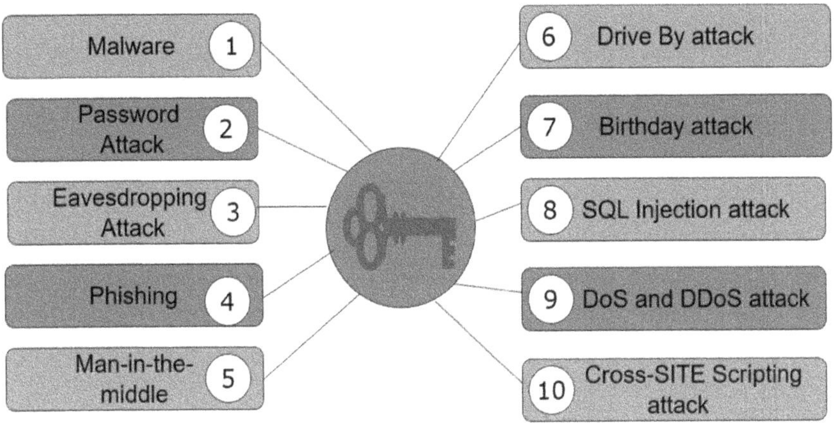

Figure 1.1 Most common cyberattacks

the greatest range of new vulnerabilities for organizations to grapple with. The sudden drastic transformations in both workplaces and their methodologies of communication while increasing dependencies towards cloud applications or virtualization products have revealed endless entry paths open to misuse by malicious people. Cybercrime harnessed profit and created a rush towards targeted hacking strategies to freeze working operations and steal sensitive information about the working framework and further use it by blackmailing in some cases. These dynamic threats have jolted organizations to be swift in the rebalancing of their cybersecurity strategies and protocols, as well as resourcefully strain the adequacy required to bolster the digital defences. COVID-19 has, undoubtedly, splashed the challenges of cyberattacks against businesses, governments, and people and justifies the crucial call to holistically take proactive measures to counter the rising tide of cyberattacks. The popular cyberattacks are shown in Figure 1.1.

Prevention of cyberattacks needs an all-round, multi-layered security strategy that can be accomplished with a combination of technical measures, strong security policies, and continuous user education and awareness programs. From the technical side, organizations should start with strong password usage and multi-factor authentication, which would prevent unauthorized access by creating a significant initial barrier. Updating software frequently and immediately implementing security patches on known vulnerabilities attackers could exploit is also essential in closing these. A properly configured firewall filters out and blocks malicious traffic, whereas intrusion detection and prevention systems proactively monitor and mitigate threats in real-time. Regular system scans using updated anti-malware and anti-virus software can detect and eliminate malicious code that somehow entered the network. Email security in the form of robust spam filters and anti-phishing protection prevents malicious emails from entering the system, thereby not compromising it. In such cases, encrypting sensitive information both in motion and at rest would be very useful in keeping information safe in case of a breach. Data back-up is another good practice where regular data is copied and archived so that, in case of a data loss incident, recoverability can take place quickly.

The other important aspect in this regard would be ongoing security awareness training because it empowers users to avoid and recognize certain potential threats, thereby strengthening the entire security posture of the organization. By adopting these multifaceted approaches, an organization can more effectively mitigate cyberattacks and then safeguard its digital assets.

1.2 Importance of Understanding Cyber Threats

Understanding cyber threats is no longer just a nice-to-have but a necessity in today's connected world. The increased use of digital technologies has resulted in an enormous and very complex attack surface that malicious actors-explicitly, individual hackers, but also sophisticated nation-state groups-can exploit. Successful attacks can be calamitous to people, organizations, governments, or critical infrastructure. Understanding the changing nature, techniques, and motivations behind these threats is of paramount importance in developing effective cybersecurity strategies and protecting our digital assets. In an increasingly digital world, it has now become an immediate need to comprehend and mitigate proliferating cyber threats. As the scale and interconnection of reliance on digital technologies escalate, malicious actors with more sophisticated attack vectors targeting personal, organizational, and national assets have grown at exponential scales. The ability to understand how, why, and what shape these cyber threats are taking allows for robust proactive cybersecurity strategies towards safeguarding digital infrastructure, sensitive data, and critical operations in the event that such a cyber breach is effective and brings ruinous effects of disruption and intrusion.

With digital technologies permeating nearly every aspect of human life, the significance of understanding cyber threats in today's interconnected world cannot be overemphasized. Cyber threats are malicious activities that target digital systems, networks, and data in order to compromise their security, integrity, and availability. As dependence on technology increases across different sectors, it will be imperative that individuals, organizations, and even governments be able to spot, understand, and reduce them.

1.2.1 The growing digital realm

The rapid evolution of digital technology has created an extremely complex web of devices, systems, and platforms all interdependent with each other.

Innovations such as cloud computing, IoT, AI, and blockchain revolutionize industries one after another, yet the growth in digital also becomes an opportunity for cybercriminals. Individual hackers to state-sponsored groups use innovative ways to crack into vulnerabilities and breach systems and steal sensitive data or disrupt important infrastructure. Cyber threat understanding will empower stakeholders to position themselves better before evolving tactics and techniques. An example of a new form of cyberattack includes ransomware-as-a-service and advanced persistent threats (APTs). A study of such phenomena can guide cybersecurity professionals on how to establish more effective defense mechanisms and proactive strategies for minimizing risk.

1.2.2 Financial and business repercussions

These result in profound economic losses. When one suffers an experienced breach of personal information, he might incur exorbitant damages or have valuable intellectual properties stolen, such that operational loss also results as services cannot take place. There have been estimative projections whereby current studies projected global cybercrimes to range in the trillions every year, among other severe losses that firms or organizations that lose the hack lose their trust. Therefore, organizations ought to understand cyber threats so that they can take measures to protect their assets and ensure the continuity of business. Through vulnerable targets and countermeasures that will effectively mitigate these risks, attacks are less likely to happen. Moreover, a culture of cybersecurity can foster within such organizations, bringing employees as a part of the defense line against phishing and social engineering attacks.

Cyber threats are one of the significant risks to national security as well as infrastructure. Presently, sectors like power grids, transportation systems, financial institutions, and healthcare facilities depend more and more on digital networks, making these areas attractive sites for cyberattacks. A critical infrastructure attack will have far-reaching consequences, ranging from widespread disruptions to economic instability and even human life loss. Governments need to understand and deal with cyber threats in order to protect national interests. This is done by spending on cybersecurity research, developing public-private partnerships, and building robust policies that handle emerging risks. International cooperation must also be realized to counter cross-border cybercrime and set up norms for responsible behavior in cyberspace. While organizations and the government have huge roles to protect themselves from the cyber threats, the individual plays a significant part in protecting oneself and one's digital footprint as well. As most cyber thieves rely on human behavior, such as phishing, identity theft, and malware distributions, understanding their nature can aid in safer Internet practices, using strong passwords, and enabling multi-factor authentication, amongst others.

Cybersecurity education and awareness programs are for individuals with knowledge and skills on how to conduct themselves safely online. Educated users are well-equipped to be able to spot and respond appropriately to cyber threats, thereby adding to personal safety and contributing more broadly to resilience in the digital ecosystem. This calls for continuous learning to keep pace with the evolving landscape of cyber threats. Cybercriminals continuously improve their tools and techniques, while traditional security controls become insufficient for protection. A well-informed cybersecurity professional and researcher about the latest trends, vulnerabilities, and attack vectors will formulate innovative solutions that counter new emergent threats. Effective cybersecurity should be multidisciplinary. Ideas from psychology, sociology, and economics can further elucidate why cybercriminals commit crimes or how they behave, helping to develop the best prevention and response strategies. Understanding the multilevel approach to cyber threats requires collaboration between these disciplines.

2 Fundamentals of Cyberattacks

Abstract: Cyberattacks have become a pervasive threat in the digital age, targeting individuals, organizations, and governments worldwide. Understanding their fundamentals is crucial for developing effective defense mechanisms. This chapter explores the various types of cyberattacks, including malware, phishing, denial-of-service (DoS), and advanced persistent threats (APTs). It also examines the evolution of cyber threats, highlighting how tactics have adapted to technological advancements. Additionally, the study identifies key actors involved in cyber warfare, such as independent hackers, organized cybercriminal groups, and nation-state-sponsored entities. By analyzing these elements, this research provides insights into the ever-changing landscape of cybersecurity threats and the necessity for proactive security strategies.

Keywords: Cyberattacks, Cyber threats, Hacking techniques, Cybercrime, Cyber operations

2.1 Types of Cyberattacks

Cyberattacks happen by exploiting weaknesses in software, hardware, and human behavior about digital systems so that malicious activities can be reached. These are weaknesses in codes, insecure configuration of networks, or susceptibility to a social engineering scheme. The unauthorized access, operational disruption, information theft, and system damage caused by attackers are mostly achieved through means such as malware (viruses, worms, ransomware), phishing, denial-of-service attacks, and SQL injection. To effectively develop a defensive strategy, these basic attack vectors and mechanisms are to be well understood for better mitigation of risks from cyber threats. Attack vectors are actually methods or pathways that an attacker takes to achieve unauthorized access in a system.

There are so many attack vectors. Some common attack vectors are described in the following sections.

2.1.1 Malware

This generally describes the variety of programs and code designed, programmed, and used with the intention to harm any computer systems, servers, clients, or networks. There are various classifications of malicious programs, such as malware viruses, worms, Trojans, ransomware, and spyware, designed to target any vulnerability, steal sensitive information, cause the operations to fail, or otherwise gain unauthorized access. In recent times, the dependence on interconnected digital systems has made malware the most popular threat, posing significant and far-reaching risks for individuals, business organizations, and governments. Technological advancements have also enhanced the sophistication and diversity of malware threats, thus necessitating powerful cybersecurity measures and close surveillance to prevent their respective impacts on society. Malware exhibits several key characteristics that distinguish it from legitimate software. It may be characterized by malicious intention, as intended to cause destruction, disrupt performance, or perhaps steal sensitive data. It, in most instances, tries to gain unauthorized access to systems or information by avoiding security methods. Most strains of malware contain the ability to replicate, resulting in the spreading of the malware between systems and exaggerating its harmful effects. To evade discovery and removal, malware has been known to incorporate mechanisms for evasion, concealing its existence within the infected environment. Some of these variants are also designed for persistence, which enables them to survive on a system even after attempts to delete them. All these features make malware a serious and persistent threat to digital security. Cyberattacks come in many forms with different characteristics and objectives. Malware is constantly changing, with new variants and modes of attack coming up every time.

However, there are some common types of malware that form the basis of many cyberattacks.

2.1.1.1 Viruses

Viruses are one of the most common and widespread kinds of malware: they are quite dangerous to the computer system and are usually self-replicating software that attaches to legitimate software and files, either without the explicit permission of a user or with any apparent knowledge of attaching. When any infected file runs, the code of the virus is activated to spread and continue infecting files and programs throughout the system. This mechanism of propagation allows viruses to spread rapidly, thus compromising the integrity and security of the entire system. The majority of viruses spread once the user has opened an infected file or is running a malicious program. But there are also some sophisticated viruses that might utilize weaknesses in certain software in order to install themselves on a computer and propagate themselves without user involvement. Once inside the system, it can conduct an unlimited range of malicious activity that includes theft of data and system disruption or installation of more malware, the creation of botnets to make further attacks

2.1.1.2 Worms

Unlike viruses, the worm is a self-replicating program. These can cross a network all by themselves. It does not necessarily need human intervention to work on a machine. Worms are able to take advantage of operating system weaknesses, application weaknesses, or network protocols in order to multiply rapidly. In most cases, worms acquire unauthorized access through software flaws in computers and even servers by just scanning open ports or unpatched vulnerabilities. Once a worm has established its presence, it can then use this access to reproduce itself, searching for other open systems and infecting them as well. The self-replicating characteristic enables worms to rapidly spread throughout networks that are highly interconnected, thus causing widespread disruption and havoc. The fact that worms do not require user involvement in the infection process makes them very insidious because they can spread silently and undetected, compromising the security of systems at scale before their presence is even known.

2.1.1.3 Trojans

These are a form of malware especially devious, disguising themselves as legitimate software, tricking the user into installing them. After being installed, a Trojan can execute a wide variety of malicious activities, such as stealing sensitive data, installing other payloads of malware, or allowing the attacker remote access to the system. The attacker can gain access to the system, sometimes unnoticed, and use it as a foothold for further exploitation. Since Trojans use social engineering techniques to trick people into letting them in, this danger is also regarded as one of the most damaging because it surpasses the capabilities of most standard protection systems. Because they act as well-known apps, they are challenging to detect and remove from the system without endangering the availability, confidentiality, and integrity of the compromised system.

2.1.1.4 Ransomware

Ransomware is the most insidious malware, threatening both individuals and businesses and organizations. The malware encrypts the files of the victim and renders them inaccessible, thus holding the data hostage. Then, it demands a ransom in cryptocurrency form in exchange for the decryption key that would be given to access the encrypted files. Ransomware attacks can have financially devastating consequences, disrupting critical operations and financially harming the institution, and compromising sensitive or proprietary information. Complete control of the decryption key by the attacker gives tremendous leverage that compels victims often to pay the ransom or risk losing critical data. The rise of ransomware has become a global concern, as the sophisticated variants are targeting almost all systems and industries, thereby further increasing the need for robust cybersecurity measures and incident response planning.

2.1.1.5 Spyware

Spyware is software maliciously designed to steal a user's information surreptitiously and silently. The collection of spywares, while invisibly monitoring the activities that may involve keystrokes, browsing history, or even financial transactions, could easily add up to massive personal and confidential information. After it has acquired such data, the spyware transfers this to the attacker, who uses such data to pursue all kinds of evil motives. It could involve identity theft, financial fraud, or blackmail. The stealthy nature of spyware and the way it has managed to infiltrate itself into systems has made this kind of malware highly insidious and dangerous and highly threatening for one's privacy, security, and digital well-being.

Spyware can even be used by the attacker for remote access to and control over the infected device, thereby gaining access to additional malicious activities like opening sensitive files and monitoring live feeds from the webcams and microphones and also hijacking a device for involvement in large-scale cyberattacks, such as a distributed denial-of-service assault.

2.1.1.6 Adware

Even though it is not always malicious, adware can still pose significant threats to its users. Usually, adware programs show plenty of intrusive and unwanted ads on a user's computer, creating hassle while working on or browsing a computer. Some adware is also created for stealthy observation of the user's browsing behaviour, where it will collect personal details like browsing history, search queries, and even financial information. This information can thus be used for targeted ads but can be misused in more disastrous ways, such as identity theft or financial fraud. The subtlety and stealth of adware makes it one of the most malicious forms of malware, as it silently enters a system to collect the user's information without their permission or cognizance. Apart from consuming the user's device performance, adware can consume the system resources and thus slow down its performance. There is an extreme need for the proper use of cybersecurity, the use of genuine antivirus software, and the proper installation of third-party applications.

2.1.1.7 Rootkits

A rootkit is an insidious malware tool whose objective is to conceal other malicious presences in the system. This means they are capable of altering the operating system in order to mask both their existence and that of other malware applications. The stealthy nature of rootkits means that it becomes impossible to detect them for the user, bypassing all the traditional security measures. As such, it remains a threat to system integrity and security because they mask malicious software activity. With this feature, attackers are in a better position to remain undetected, maintaining control over the compromised system, leading to further exploitation and data breaches. Another form of use is to establish backdoors, enable remote access, and allow other malware to install itself on the infected system; this grants an attacker persistent, surreptitious control over an infected system. This makes rootkits very difficult to detect and eradicate and, therefore, represents a serious threat to the confidentiality, integrity, and availability of targeted systems.

2.1.1.8 Botnets

A botnet is a large collection of compromised computers controlled by one malicious actor. These connected devices, referred to as "bots," can be used by the hacker to perform all sorts of nefarious activities. Botnets can be used to orchestrate devastating distributed denial-of-service attacks, send spam messages that overwhelm systems and networks, or steal sensitive data from infected systems. The sheer scale and coordinated nature of botnets pose a major threat, bringing potential disruption, financial loss, and data breaches. Protecting against botnets calls for multifaceted efforts, from robust security measures to educate the user to coordinated efforts from cybersecurity professionals, law enforcement, and internet service providers. Besides being used in malicious ways against a person's or business's device, botnets can be deployed for other malign activities like the mining of cryptocurrency. The bots drain the infected resources and may mean considerable expense on the victim's side. In the dark web, botnets could be rented and sold to relatively less technically savvy hackers to allow those vast networks they build for various criminal aims.

2.1.1.9 Keylogger

A keylogger is malware that records the keystroke activities of a computer user. Some examples of confidential information include passwords, logins, credit cards, and other highly classified information, all recorded from keystrokes without any notification. The software quietly works in the background and sends this data into some log without your consent. The keyloggers pose one of the severe threats to one's privacy and security because this collected data might be used in identity theft or financial fraud against a person or for other mischievous use. To save against keyloggers, alertness, antivirus software use, and extreme caution when shared or public use of devices will be necessary. To further reduce the risks, users should monitor their accounts regularly for suspicious activity, change passwords frequently, and consider the use of hardware-based security measures such as physical locks or input devices that encrypt.

2.1.1.10 Logic Bombs

It is a particularly malevolent form of malicious code placed secretly within an otherwise legitimate program or software application. Unlike some other forms of malware, whose effects are manifest immediately, this type of attack is designed to lie dormant and wait for particular predefined conditions or triggers to become active, whereby it will cause a harmful or destructive action. Triggers for logic bombs may include, but are not limited to: date and time-based; on occurrence of certain events; in the presence of specific system states or conditions. Upon meeting these conditions, it is able to conduct all kinds of malicious activity that might involve destroying or overwriting important files, disabling key systems, or permitting unauthorized access into the environment it compromised. Logic bombs are insidious because they may remain dormant for a long time, making the users and security measures feel at ease. After the predetermined conditions are met, the logic bomb may spring into action and cause significant and often catastrophic damage to the affected systems and networks. Indeed, the only defence against all these threats would be a round-the-clock monitoring of system activity, software updates, and comprehensive security measures to detect and prevent the introduction of malicious code into critical systems, and also proper employee training and awareness programmes would play a crucial role in the identification and mitigation of risks associated with logic bombs and all other advanced cyber threats.

2.1.2 Phishing

Phishing is a new form of increasingly common cyberattacks in which a malicious actor imitates a legitimate person or organization usually via email, websites, and text messages that are used to make users reveal sensitive information such as user names, passwords, credit card information, or even social security numbers. These attacks take advantage of human frailties and very often use clever social engineering movements to get users to take security-compromising actions, for example, opening malicious links in e-mails or attachments that happen to be infected or providing passwords or other identifying information on a scam website. Impacts of a phishing attack include identity theft, financial loss, data breaches, and malware infection that can create wide-ranging and significant impacts on the victims. Attackers usually create very convincing fake versions of legitimate websites or emails, making it extremely difficult for even the most vigilant users to detect the scam. Other variations of phishing include spear phishing and whaling. These usually target specific people or organizations that make it all the more probable when an attack is successful. It targets big shots like executives. Phishing is defended by the multifaceted approach, which commingles technological measures such as spam filters and anti-phishing software with comprehensive user education about the detection and avoidance of suspicious communications. User vigilance in checking the validity of any email or message requesting personal information by examining the sender's address and exercising great caution about clicking on links and opening attachment items from unknown sources will help. Software and the operating system can also be updated regularly to avoid vulnerabilities for phishing exploits.

2.1.3 Denial-of-Service and Distributed Denial-of-Service Attacks

A Denial-of-Service attack or a Distributed Denial-of-Service attack refers to the malicious activity aimed at rendering an assigned server, service, or network functionless through flooding the intended user of that resource with internet traffic, which it has to sort out and hence will make it unable to deliver any services for which it is maintained. This way, the target of DoS attacks actually consumes the target's available bandwidth or system resources/ applications, leaving no access for actual users to make use of it. DDoS attacks begin from a singular source, as opposed to using multiple compromised machines, usually in the form of a botnet, to intensify impact and make attacks harder to contain. The robust network security measures, traffic monitoring, and incident response plans should be in place to quickly identify and mitigate the attack. In a Denial-of-Service attack, malicious traffic will come from one source, probably a compromised computer or server. The attacker would flood the target with a huge volume of unnecessary requests over the target's capacity to manage legitimate traffic; thus, this would shut down the target. This can shut down the access to legitimate users through the overpowering of target resources. While DoS attacks from a single source are much easier to execute, they are in general easier to mitigate and defend against than the more complex distributed version, often referred to as a Distributed Denial-of-Service attack.

DDoS attacks make use of the compromised machines in a botnet to amplify their attack. Compromised machines are controlled secretly by the attackers, usually not known to their owners, while they are flooding the target by sending traffic to it from all the compromised machines in unison. This distributed technique makes DDoS attacks hard to defend since blocking one source does not make the attack go away. The sheer volume of traffic coming out of a botnet is readily capable of flooding the most resiliently designed network infrastructures, effectively excluding legitimate users of the service or system targeted in the DDoS attack. DDoS attacks can sometimes be nearly impossible to stop; the nature of the attack tends to ensure it is nearly impossible to locate individual sources from thousands of machines that are geographically diverse.

Some of the commonly used methods by DoS and DDoS attacks are the following.

- ***UDP floods:*** These involve flooding a target system with a massive volume of UDP packets to its randomly selected ports. This prevents it from further handling legitimate traffic.
- ***SYN floods:*** A form of an attack that overwhelms the system's resources as the target sends an incomplete request to initiate the connection.
- ***HTTP flood:*** It includes flooding the targeted system with millions of HTTP requests, mostly from legitimate traffic origins, in an attempt to overburden its capacity.
- ***ICMP flood:*** This is usually done by transmitting millions of ICMP echo requests towards the target in order to drain its network resources and bandwidth.

These methods overwhelm and deny a server, service, or network its accessibility to its regular users. DoS and DDoS attacks may have severe consequences, from partial to significant disruptions of services to temporary or permanent losses of reputations, money, or leakage of data. For businesses, a successful DDoS attack could disrupt online operations, affecting customer service, sales, and productivity. In critical infrastructure, like healthcare or emergency services, the DDoS attack may be life-threatening.

2.1.4 Man-in-the-Middle Attacks

A Man-in-the-Middle attack is a form of cyberattack, whereby the attacker intercepts and may alter communication between two parties who believe that they are communicating with each other directly. So, it puts the attacker in a middle position on the channel of communication without being noticed by both parties communicating. That will enable the attacker to intercept conversations for his malicious use, steal sensitive information, manipulate data, or introduce malicious code. This attack exploits vulnerabilities of various communication protocols and can target different layers within the network stack. One good example is how an attacker gets to intercept your traffic on a public Wi-Fi. By placing oneself between a user and the access point of Wi-Fi, this attacker can monitor data transmitted between these two, for instance, the login credentials and browsing history along with financial details.

Several common techniques used in man-in-the-middle attacks include:

• ***ARP spoofing:*** Send wrong ARP messages, which allow the target computer's MAC address association with some hacker's MAC by the MAC association process. It gains access to intercept packets it intends to receive instead to hackers MAC.

• ***DNS spoofing:*** It is a DNS record manipulation activity by the attackers to redirect users to forged websites that exactly look like their original counterparts to steal login details and other important information.

• ***Session hijacking:*** An attacker steals a user's session ID, thereby allowing him to impersonate the user and gain unauthorized access to the user's online accounts. The hijacker stole a session ID owned by another, enabling the hijacker to access the online accounts of the victim with someone else's identity.

• ***SSL/TLS stripping:*** An attacker intercepts HTTPS traffic and downgrades it to HTTP. This way, the encryption is removed, allowing the attacker to listen in on the communication and perhaps compromise the confidentiality and integrity of the data being exchanged.

2.1.5 SQL Injection

SQL injection is a web application security vulnerability related to inserting malicious SQL code into the input fields of an application, manipulating the query executed by the application over its database. It may allow hackers to gain unauthorized access to the sensitive data that might have been hidden inside the database, including data breaches, data manipulation, and even complete control over the database server. The problem arises due to a weakness of not properly sanitizing and validating user-supplied input before passing it in to be executed by the SQL query. Thus, by entering input with malicious SQL code in it, attackers can successfully inject it, and the database executes this as code, which then provides an unauthorized person the unintended ability and power over the database.

Some common techniques used in these attacks include:

• ***Tautologies:*** Adding code that always evaluates to true, making it possible for an attacker to bypass any authentication checks placed in front of the system. For example, entering the SQL statement " ' OR '1'='1'" into a username field effectively bypasses login credentials.

• ***Union-based attacks:*** Exploiting the UNION keyword to merge the result set of a legitimate SQL query with that of an attack query. This will help in retrieving information from other tables that the attacker should not be able to view.

• ***Blind SQL injection:*** This method of attack exploits minute variations in the behavior of the application to draw information about the structure of the database or the data, without access to the actual results. This can be used slowly to construct sensitive information about the target system. This allows for the gradual piecing together of sensitive information about the target system.

• ***Stored procedures:*** Injecting malicious code within pre-compiled SQL queries stored on the database server can then be run with elevated privilege; this may then lead to the full system being compromised.

2.1.6 Zero-Day Exploits

A zero-day exploit is one that takes advantage of a weakness in software on which the maker or vendor doesn't know of yet. Thus, there will be no patching available to remove the vulnerability—the attacks are rather dangerous. In fact, it's called zero-day because this is the point at which the vendor has no days to mitigate the vulnerability that's been used. Zero-day exploits, on the other hand, pose a great concern for attackers due to their extreme difficulty in discovery and defense mechanisms. Traditional means of security, such as using antivirus or firewalls and others, are nearly ineffective in combating this because they detect attacks through known patterns or signatures from malicious activity, and by default, zero-day exploits are newly introduced and thereby not detectable.

2.1.7 Social Engineering

Social engineering is a manipulation technique that exploits human psychology to make individuals reveal confidential information or do things that compromise security. Social engineering does not depend on technical hacking but rather uses psychological manipulation to take advantage of the human tendencies of trusting, being helpful, and fear. The attacker will usually assume the identity of trusted figures, such as IT personnel or authority figures, to gain the victim's confidence. They could even apply all types of social engineering, such as through phishing emails, pretexting that creates false scenarios, baiting that will make an attack give in because it wants the item that he will bait you with, quid pro quo by providing them something with information on his computer and other important files in it, and then there's tailgating—physical unauthorized entry to their space.

Social engineering attacks can have an important impact. Data breaches, financial losses, identity theft, and reputational damage are common results of a social engineering attack. Security awareness training and proper security practices protect against social engineering attacks. Train employees to be aware of requests that seem suspicious, verify who is asking for information, and not click on links or open attachments from people they do not know. Organizations should have strong security protocols in place, such as multi-factor authentication, access controls, and regular security audits, to minimize the risk of successful social engineering attacks.

2.2 Evolution of Cyber Threats

The rapid spread of the digital landscape and the threats hiding within it have increased correspondingly. Cyber threats over time have evolved steadily in the cybersecurity landscape, with new types of increasingly sophisticated attacks over the years. The overall nature and impact of these threats have grown in complexity, scale, and depth to pose huge challenges for individuals, organizations, and governments. Different evolution factors of the cyber threats relate to the growth in technology developments, increased dependencies on digital and internet systems, sophistication of a threat actor group, and continually expanding attack surfaces. Cyber hackers, nation states, and hacktivists make up the whole evolving threat group that is making new vulnerabilities identified and new and innovative techniques available to infiltrate and disrupt such computer-based systems and networks. This landscape is no longer a static battlefield that requires defenders to continuously adapt strategies and technologies for an edge on the curve. The emergence of new technologies like artificial intelligence, cloud computing, and the Internet of Things, which have changed vulnerabilities and attack vectors, requires addressing them by the cybersecurity professional. Effective cybersecurity measures demand a holistic and proactive approach covering as many aspects as possible in technical, organizational, and human terms to protect against the emerging risk of cyber threats.

The initial cyber threats were not sophisticated. Initially, these cyber threats came from the curiosities or the pranks of the hackers. Initial attacks on the systems focused more on breaking into systems and defacing sites without significant financial or strategic motives. With advancements in technology and an increasing dependence on digital systems, so did the motivation and sophistication of the attackers. Cybercrime is now a full-time industry and an enterprise involving powerful organized criminal groups and even nation-state actors. The growing dependency on digitalization in every single aspect of life, from the most social contacts to critical infrastructures, has elevated the sense of urgency for strong cybersecurity measures. Cybersecurity is driven by complex dynamics between attackers, defenders, and users—where each continually adjusts their approach and strategy to stay ahead in the game.

One of the major factors contributing to the transformation of the cyber threat landscape is the fast and exponential expansion of technology and, consequently, the digital realm. The more devices, systems, and services that become ever more interconnected, the more explosive the potential attack surface for the malicious actor has become. New technologies and technological trends- For example, transformative new technologies that are known today include IoT and cloud computing and present numerous new risks of vulnerability through which cybercriminals could exploit to ruthlessly manipulate systems. Some new technological capabilities also introduce risks related to issues that could benefit them by posing increased and complicated forms of cybersecurity challenges. This made the landscape of cybersecurity highly complex, dynamic, and very changing with which it has always proved to be the battlefield on which defenders had constantly adapted their strategies and solutions for defence against ever-gaining curve for effective protection of digital assets and critical infrastructure.

The development of cyber threats has characterized some important trends which contribute to its complexity and the gravity and impact as well:

- ***Sophisticated attacks:*** Sophisticated attacks are experienced, which often involve using state-of-the-art techniques such as polymorphic malware, rootkits, and even exploit zero-day attacks.

- ***Targeted:*** The threat actor has shifted more towards targeted assaults, away from broadly indiscriminate ones. In turn, these enemies can accomplish a better effect as they are known to carefully look at their targets and calibrate attacks toward the best and maximum impact they can get with the assault they are launching.

- ***Automation and scale:*** With automated tools and techniques, attackers could launch large-scale attacks with much easier and minimal effort as it becomes a relatively easy operation to execute some complex, coordinated campaigns that will overwhelm and compromise a vast number of systems and networks.

- ***Exploitation of emerging technologies:*** As new technologies, such as cloud computing, mobile devices, and the Internet of Things, continuously change the nature of the digital landscape, there has been nothing but a flurry of activity with attackers identifying, exploiting, and taking advantage of all the vulnerabilities innate in these developing systems, seemingly outpacing the efforts made by defenders in securing them. Cybercriminals capitalized on the wide adoption of these emerging technologies, using their inherent weaknesses as a springboard for increasingly more sophisticated and widespread attacks.

- ***Collaboration and information sharing:*** The cybercriminals have become better at collaboration and information sharing, tactics, and resources, thereby increasing their combined strength and making it tougher for security professionals to track, predict, and mitigate these threats. Dark web forums, underground marketplaces, and peer-to-peer networks have all served as facilitators of the exchange of hacking tools, exploit kits, and shared strategies among threat actors.

- ***Diversity in motives:*** The motives of cyber-attacks also diversified into monetary gain and espionage, ideological or political, even purely disruptive in nature. So, the threat actors might be motivated through personal, organizational, or national interests, thereby making it hard to predict or counter their activity.

An ever more interconnected systems and data will, therefore provide a fertile breeding ground for cyberattacks. However, to curtail these risks, organizations as well as the individuals must, therefore, embark on proactive, multi-layered security measures, such as applying effective security measures including updating their software regularly, ensuring two-factor authentication, network monitoring, as well as adequate investment in holistic security awareness for the employees who should identify and act accordingly to thwart possible threats. Investment in comprehensive security awareness training for employees will enable them to recognize and respond appropriately to threats. Staying updated on new emerging cyber threats is also vital by reading industry reports and government advisories to prepare and predict the attack vectors that might be new. With all these robust security measures, you will be better placed to gain valuable insights about the evolving threat landscape and keep in step with it, securing your digital assets and critical infrastructure.

2.3 Key Actors: Hackers, Cybercriminals, and Nation-States

The digital realm is a complex battleground with different actors that have their reasons and capabilities in seeking control and influence. Knowledge of these major players—hackers, cybercriminals, and nation-states—is essential for understanding the dynamics of the constantly changing cyber threat landscape and, by extension, for developing adequate defense strategies. All these disparate elements, with their assorted goals—from monetary motives to political convictions—have certainly added to the complexity and intensity of the cyber threats confronting individuals, institutions, and nations. Delving into the general characteristics and actions of these top players will really help security personnel anticipate, recognize, and curtail the shifting nature of those digital threats threatening them in such an advanced time.

2.3.1 Hackers

The term hacker has evolved as time passed, from referring initially to people of great knowledge related to computer systems, often full of curiosity about technology and inspired to explore, modify, or manipulate it for whatever reason, but not without the ethical use of their capability. Some hacks are still today conducted within this boundary, yet others use those skills for wicked purposes. HACKERS can sometimes be motivated either by financial needs, political agitation, or possibly the thrill from the challenge. They can use this technical expertise for the exploitation of weaknesses, malware design, and other means of destroying systems. Based on the intentions and approach, hackers are categorized as follows:

- ***White hat hackers:*** These are ethically hacking ones known as the "white hat" hackers; they apply extensive knowledge in technical competence and knowledge in how computers work so that they detect security weaknesses for the organizations' purposes. This collaboration with these organizations and establishments usually takes the form of participation in bug bounties and penetration testing activities in order to improve the companies' overall safety and protection measures against cybercrimes. By revealing and responsibly publishing weaknesses, white hat hackers form an integral part of digital protection for clients. In so doing, they promote the online world's security.

- ***Black hat hackers:*** These are a category of rogue hackers that leverage these weaknesses, apply their technological prowess for accessing systems they shouldn't without proper authority or with a bad intent like theft or vandalism, and destroy services, primarily in furtherance of malicious objectives like money-making or propaganda. They may carry out a number of malicious activities, including malware deployment, cyber espionage, or disruption attacks, with the aim of achieving their evil objectives at the expense of their victims.

- ***Gray hat hackers:*** These hackers are sometimes called "gray hat" hackers and operate in the gray area between ethical and unethical practices. Their operations may sometimes reach unethical levels; however, the intent is not necessarily malicious but rather to target vulnerabilities in a system or network with the objective of bringing into the limelight security issues as opposed to benefiting from them. Gray hat hackers are in an exclusive position and use their technical skills to determine and highlight vulnerabilities with the goal of improving general security. However, their activities can still be considered illegal or unauthorized, hence creating a rather complex and nuanced landscape.

Regardless of their motives, hackers continue to represent a significant threat as they evolve with relentless determination to perfect their tactics and techniques for staying one step ahead of security measures. Therefore, this dynamic, fast-paced landscape requires organizations and individuals to stay alert, proactive, and adaptable in their pursuit of cybersecurity. They can therefore be able to better anticipate, detect, and mitigate the increasingly sophisticated cyber threats that continue to emerge by staying informed, implementing robust security protocols, and continuously enhancing their defensive capabilities.

2.3.2 Cybercriminals

They are primarily money-motivated and engage in a wide variety of illegal acts to achieve their objectives. Cybercriminals usually operate in very organized groups. These criminal syndicates frequently employ advanced skills, resources, and networks to achieve the greatest profits while minimizing law enforcement efforts. In this regard, they often have high levels of sophistication in terms of the advanced tactics and technologies that they use in their malicious activities. By working collectively in coordinated attacks, cyberhackers can build a pool of their expertise, collect intelligence, and coordinate complex, harder-to-detect attacks. Being a network-like organization, their interconnective structure allows the organization to readily change its methods upon new circumstances in an effort towards continued evolution—a formidability for individuals and organizations and generally for society as a whole. Some common tactics include:

- ***Ransomware attacks:*** These are the attacks in which cybercriminals encrypt the data and request payment from victims to release them. This could be very damaging as it affects business operations, and critical information is lost.
- ***Data breaches:*** Cyberhackers steal sensitive data, including credit card numbers and other personal information, and sell it on the black market. Consequently, this data might be used in identity theft, financial fraud, and other forms of malicious activity.
- ***Financial fraud:*** Cybercrooks manipulate web-based banking to steal money right from victims; this may sometimes have devastating implications on financial balances for both an individual and even an organization.
- ***Malware distribution:*** Cyber thieves develop and spread malware to somehow infect and control computer systems and then continue with their criminal activities.

2.3.3 Nation-state

Another significant source of cyberthreats is posed by nation-state actors, who are government-sponsored groups or intelligence agencies. In most cases, these actors are motivated by geopolitical ambitions, national security concerns, or the need to gain a strategic advantage over adversaries. They might resort to wide varieties of malpractice, for instance, conducting cyber espionage by taking sensitive information from others' databases, attacking some critical infrastructures to just bring chaos to these systems, and targeting any selected group just to fulfill strategic missions. Equipped with vast assets and capabilities, nation-state attackers can conduct increasingly complex and continuous attacks that go undetected and are unmitigated easily, posing serious threats to nation, organization, and individual security. Nation-states are a fast-growing and ever-present threat in cyberspace, and their drives are usually politics or strategic considerations, and they undertake a variety of malicious activities to include:

- ***Cyber espionage:*** This involves the theft of sensitive information that includes military plans, trade secrets, or personal data from another country or organization to give them a strategic advantage.

- ***Cyber warfare:*** Intercepting or incapacitating essential infrastructure, such as power grids, communication networks, or transportation systems, to cause chaos and instability in their adversaries.

- ***Information war:*** Use propaganda or false information on the web, break into information systems, or even edit online information for the public opinion to support and influence their policy.

- ***Economic sabotage:*** Generally, the attempt to affect an opponent's economic ability by targeting its financial system, supply chain, or intellectual property, and eventually weakening the opponent's economic position relative to itself.

Nation-states are significant in resources and expertise and therefore a potent opponent. Advanced persistent threats, in particular, are sophisticated attacks aimed at the penetration and stay for a long time in target systems without being noticed.

In such a scenario, sometimes the boundaries of these distinct actor groups overlap and interlace with each other. Hackers can be employed by or partnered with cybercriminals or nation-states. In a more complicated example, cybercriminals are known to offer their specific expertise and abilities to nations in return for attaining their specific strategic goals. Such an intricacy of webs of relationships and alliances between and among different cyber threat actors is a more difficult task to penetrate for the effective working of the general cyber threat landscape.

3 Common Types of Cyberattacks

Abstract: Cyberattacks have evolved into a major security concern, posing risks to individuals, businesses, and governments. This paper examines the most common types of cyber-attacks, including ransomware, which encrypts data for ransom; Distributed Denial-of-Service (DDoS) attacks, which overwhelm systems to cause disruption; and Advanced Persistent Threats (APTs), which involve prolonged, stealthy infiltration. Additionally, it explores phishing attacks that manipulate users into revealing sensitive information, zero-day exploits that target undiscovered vulnerabilities, and insider threats originating from within organizations. Understanding these threats is essential for developing effective cybersecurity strategies to mitigate risks and enhance digital resilience.

Keywords: Cybersecurity threats, Ransomware, Phishing attacks, Zero-day exploits, Insider threats

3.1 Ransomware Attacks

The cybersecurity landscape has witnessed an evolution of threats at a pace that has outpaced its maturation process; the advancement and sophistication of more complex and powerful attacks are rampant. Cybercrime organizations, nation-state actors, and other malevolent forces have increased the sophistication and seriousness of cyber threats significantly. Ransomware attacks are the most prevalent and sophisticated forms of threats that can be seen in the digital world, attacking not only people and businesses but also critical infrastructure. The malware attacks encrypt the data, and this makes it impossible for the victim to access. In return for providing the decryption key, the attackers demand ransom in cryptocurrency. Ransomware attacks have catastrophic effects on an organization, which can include the loss of data, financial loss, reputational damage, and disruption of crucial services. One of the greatest cybersecurity threats seen in recent times is ransomware, with hackers continually creating new variants and ways to avoid detection while maximizing profits. This impacts their operations in different ways, disabling companies and health facilities while simultaneously disrupting important services and infrastructures of governmental institutions. Since the ransomware is evolving daily, organizations must take their level of cybersecurity precautions by remaining vigilant to such malicious activities.

Ransomware attacks usually involve several different stages:

(1) Infection: There are several modes of infection via which ransomware gains access into a system, such as phishing emails, attachments, or a vulnerability in any software. Those infection vectors mean malware gets some initial access in the target system.

(2) Encryption: The ransomware program, having established itself inside the system, goes ahead and starts encrypting files, folders, or entire hard drives in order to keep data inaccessible for the user. The encryption mechanism forms the essential core of any ransomware attack since it demands money from a victim in lieu of releasing data back.

(3) Data recovery: The attacker will hand over the decryption key in case the ransom is paid. It is then that the victim can regain access to their encrypted data. There is no assurance, however, that the attacker will stick to their word, and some victims never get their data recovered even after paying the ransom.

(4) Ransom demand: After this, the attacker comes out with a ransom note that states that a decryption key is needed in exchange for a payment. The ransom demanded may be from hundreds of dollars to millions, depending on the extent and effects of the attack.

(5) Payment pressure: The cybercriminals usually send threatening messages asking the victim to pay the ransom within a tight deadline or delete the encrypted file if the victim does not send the money to them. It is done by the cybercrooks to compel the victim to pay the money by increasing desperation and urgency to meet the requirement.

There are various types of ransomwares, which differ from one another in their characteristics and ways of attacking. These include:

(a) Crypto-ransomware: This is the most common form, encrypting data and demanding money for its release. It is a ransomware that encrypts files and folders, which can only be accessed after paying the ransom for the decryption key.

(b) Locker ransomware: Locker ransomware will lock out users from the complete system and any data or programs. It steals control of a system and begins demanding money for reopening access.

(c) Leakware: This ransomware type steals users' confidential information and warns that it will publish it if one doesn't pay the ransom. Here, an attacker gains the users' confidential information and uses it as a bargaining tool for extorting its victim.

(d) Ransomware-as-a-Service: This model is one where ransomware tools and infrastructure can be rented or leased by cybercriminals; this makes it much easier for not-so-technically-savvy cyber attackers to do their thing. It has lowered the bar to engaging in ransomware attacks.

Protecting an organization from ransomware attacks must be at a multi-layered level:

(a) Security software: Upgrading installed security software and running frequent scans will alert one of the probabilities and delete ransomware before it encrypts any data. Strong antivirus, antimalware, and firewall software can protect an organization from ransomware attacks remarkably.

(b) User education: It is also a very important requirement to educate the users on ransomware threats and how not to get infected. This can include training in the identification of phishing e-mails, how to avoid dubious links and attachments, and best practices in passwords. This is a long way to mitigating ransomware attacks by keeping the employees alert and reporting any suspicious activities.

(c) Regular backups: Critical data needs to be created and regularly backed up to aid in the recovery process if the attack takes place. The location where the backup will be kept needs to be not accessible through the infected system but rather a separate, offsite location that the ransomware would not be able to access and could encrypt. Therefore, it could restore from the clean copy while minimizing damage.

Software updates are an ongoing process to patch operating systems and applications that are potentially exploited by ransomware. Therefore, maintaining up-to-date security patches in all systems will keep the cybercriminals from taking advantage of any known vulnerabilities. Incident Response Plan Organizations can immediately and effectively act during a ransomware attack in the event there is a well-formulated incident response plan. Therefore, this step must clearly define every move to make, the various roles, and the individual responsibilities with their communication procedures in order for effective coordination.

Ransomware attacks have proven to be one of the more significant and quickly evolving threats for individuals and organizations. However, with an effective set of robust security measures implemented, including data backups, current software and security solutions, and continuous user education, individuals and organizations can protect themselves from the effects of such attacks. In fact, staying up-to-date on the latest ransomware trends and attack vectors is of utmost importance since cybercriminals are continually evolving new tactics and techniques for penetrating systems and holding data hostage. A proactive, multilayered approach to cybersecurity is in order when facing such an evolving threat landscape.

3.2 Distributed Denial-of-Service (DDoS)

Distributed Denial-of-Service attack: A Distributed Denial-of-Service attack refers to an illicit attempt to incapacitate the regular flow of traffic or operations of any targeted server, service, or network by bringing it under its full assault of Internet traffic. DDoS achieves this incapacitation by using the compromised computer system, commonly called "bots" or "zombies," to serve as attack traffic sources. Such systems, which usually carry malware and are operated from a centralized command-and-control server controlled by the attacker, send a mix of malicious traffic that overwhelms the targeted resource and denies legitimate users from accessing it. However, the effects could be as benign as a periodic service outage resulting from a low-level DDoS attack or of significant financial nature, reputational damage, as well as breaking down critical infrastructures and some essential services for people. Some DDoS attacks can truly threaten organizations, as well as individuals, mainly because they incapacitate access and use of valued online resources as well as pertinent services. Effective mitigation strategies such as network infrastructure improvements, traffic filtering, and cloud-based DDoS protection will be necessary in order to prevent these attacks from affecting the continued availability and reliability of online systems and services.

The attack primarily utilizes these exploited systems to cause various types of malicious traffic toward the target and designed to disrupt its operations:

These may include,

• ***UDP floods:*** Sends huge volumes of UDP packets, which overwhelms network capacities, wasting bandwidth, thus bringing about complete disruption of a service or the overall network being congested.

• ***SYN floods:*** A form of DoS attack, which is exploited by sending numerous SYN requests but not completing the connection. It would consume all server resources of the target, like memory and CPU, and make it impossible to allow legitimate connections to be established.

• ***HTTP floods:*** Deluge the target's web server with enormous HTTP requests and overburden it with a huge amount of processing requirements in order to severely impair its functioning, thereby sometimes creating a total outage of service.

- ***ICMP flooding:*** Targeted ICMP echo requests consume system resources as well as bandwidth of the network and actually deny access to legitimate users as well as services.

In doing so, this type of DDoS may disrupt the proper functioning of any targeted server, service, or network, thereby hampering or wholly preventing legitimate access to the resources targeted. Results of such an attack can result in minor or major inconveniences, all the way through to financial costs, reputational damage, up to and even including disruption to critical infrastructure as well as loss of essential services. Effective mitigation strategies involving network infrastructure enhancement, traffic filtering, and even cloud-based protection against DDoS attacks make it possible for the defense system to be established and ensure these systems and online services remain as available and accessible as possible to users.

DDoS attacks may be classified based on the layer in the OSI model they are targeting. There are these:

- ***Volume-based attacks:*** Volume-based attacks flood the targeted system with immense amounts of traffic that consume both bandwidth and overwhelm network infrastructure. Examples include the use of UDP floods, overwhelming the target's network capacity by sending large volumes of UDP packets, and ICMP floods, which flood the target with ICMP echo requests, both consuming system resources and bandwidth. The others, including the DNS amplification attack, fall under volume-based attacks where compromised servers can use them to multiply the original volume of the traffic sent to thousands of times what the attacker asked for.

- ***Protocol attacks:*** Protocol attacks include exploitation of weaknesses in network protocols, including TCP and UDP. These attacks drain server resources. For example, the SYN flood exploits the TCP handshake process by submitting SYN requests in large volumes without completing the connections, thereby using up the server's resources on the target, including memory and CPU. These are protocol-based, with an attacker sending a set of fragmented UDP packets to the victim such that his reassembling and processing of traffic become overloaded.

- ***Application-layer attacks:*** The goal of application-layer attacks is on specific applications or services like web servers and databases. An HTTP flood involves a massive number of HTTP requests towards the target's web server that would overload the system with demands to process them, thereby disabling the normal flow of operations. A Slowloris attack is about maintaining several incomplete HTTP connections in order not to allow the server to process the legitimate requests.

For successful protection against DDoS attacks, a very complete and multi-layered system of defense needs to be provided. The foremost measures are putting robust network infrastructure into place—advanced firewalls, intrusion detection and prevention systems, and load balancers help considerably in weakening the impact of DDoS attacks. The overall malicious traffic will be detected and filtered while letting legitimate access remain. In addition to fortifying the foundation of the network, applying traffic filtering techniques at the network edge is necessary. With appropriate traffic analysis and selective blocking of suspicious patterns of traffic, the organizations would not even let the malicious traffic reach the target server in order to safeguard it from a DDoS attack onslaught.

But other than the preceding, utilizing the cloud-based service for mitigating DDoS attacks offers some extra level of protection. Dedicated services will identify threats, analyze their nature, and provide real-time recommendations for the removal of threats against DDoS attacks on highly distributed infrastructures by developing complex algorithms for processing. This can be done with a well-defined and regularly tested incident response plan. This defines the steps taken, the role of key personnel in it, and the communication strategy employed during a DDoS attack. This can ensure that in case of a DDoS attack, preparedness will not allow such disruptions and ensure online services and infrastructures are up and running in a very timely manner. The seriousness of the resultant confusion and disruptions to their services makes it vital for organizations to protect themselves from this disastrous impact of DDoS attacks by implementing these comprehensive sets of mitigation strategies. There's a great necessity for robust, multi-layered, and all-around defense against persistent threat DDoS attacks. Primarily, a defense that bases its operation around advanced network infrastructures would primarily include the addition of load balancers, intrusion detection and prevention systems, as well as advanced firewalls. These systems help detect the malicious traffic, analyze it for maliciousness, selectively filter those malicious pieces, and ensure the users' continued accessibility even during heavy DDoS pressure.

The only way to defend against continuously threatening DDoS attacks would be a totally multi-level approach. But, at the base level, robust network infrastructure in terms of high-end firewalls, intrusion detection and prevention systems, and load balancers will go a long way in relieving the impacts these attacks present. These solutions will help determine malicious traffic, scan it, and filter it selectively so that continued access for legitimate users can remain unaffected even during high levels of DDoS pressure. Moreover, cloud-based DDoS mitigation services can offer an extra layer of protection that is highly scalable against large and complex attacks. Specialized DDoS mitigation services use distributed infrastructure and advanced algorithms to detect, analyze, and then mitigate real-time threats offered by DDoS in a way that makes it quite robust for organizations challenged. Organizations can expand their defense potential and ensure critical online services or infrastructure remain online by availing themselves of the vast amounts of resources and expertise cloud-based providers carry. Last, an incident response plan must be well defined and regularly tested. The steps involved in such a process, the roles of key personnel, and the kind of communication that should be involved during such times must be mentioned. In this regard, preparation with a prompt response can reduce the level of disruptions these attacks will cause to such organizations while continuing to maintain online services and access to resources. This holistic set of mitigation strategies allows organizations to protect themselves better from the disruptive impact of DDoS attacks so that their critical digital infrastructure and services continue to remain reliable and available to their users.

3.3 Advanced Persistent Threats (APTs)

Advanced Persistent Threats are perhaps the most technologically advanced forms of cyberespionage, usually created by well-capitalized nation states or sophisticated cybercrime entities. While there are opportunistic attacks seeking monetary gain in a more straightforward manner, APT attacks are characterized as having extraordinary stealth, unyielding persistence, and targeted attempts at sensitive data and critical infrastructures. Such sneaky and determined attacks are created in order to have an undetected stay for a considerable time, even sometimes for years. This makes them collect vital information, be it intellectual property, financial data, or any confidential data of a government, as long as they acquire sustained access to an organization's core infrastructure and its system. Therefore, APTs will not be based on immediate monetary benefits but, instead, focus on the process of systematic, secretive gathering of information or installing long-term access controls over the target's digital resources.

Several critical characteristics distinguish APTs from other types of cyberattacks:

- ***Specific targeting:*** APTs are targeted and well-planned operations focusing on particular organizations, individuals, or systems that contain valuable information or have access to critical infrastructure. Attackers carry out extensive research and analysis about their targets and know their vulnerabilities and entry points.
- ***Stealth and evasion:*** APTs use all sorts of highly sophisticated techniques in order to stay undetected and unobtrusive inside the target network. These tactics include custom-made malware, previously unknown vulnerabilities to

be exploited, and highly sophisticated evasion techniques that bypass security tools and monitoring.

• ***Persistence:*** APTs are designed to have a persistent and covert presence inside the target's network for long periods of time. If individual components are discovered and removed, the attackers can stay in control, including by finding ways to regain access if needed, allowing for their continued control of the compromised systems.

• ***Data exfiltration:*** Data exfiltration is the main aim of APTs, including systematic and clandestine collection of sensitive data. Such data might be intellectual property, financial records, government secrets, or any other information considered valuable for espionage, strategic advantages, or monetary gains.

• ***Advanced capabilities:*** Advanced APT actors tend to have much more extensive resources, such as highly skilled cybersecurity professionals, ample funding, and access to an array of highly sophisticated tools and techniques. They can then build and deliver malware that is very sophisticated, take advantage of the latest vulnerabilities, and execute attacks that are highly intricate and evasive, evading even the best security controls.

3.3.1 Stages of an APT Attack

An APT attack typically has planned stages to systematically compromise the adversary's systems and infrastructure:

• ***Reconnaissance:*** Reconnaissance involves as much time spent for the attacker, who will study details about the target organization, identifying potential weaknesses, vulnerability points, and a point of access. It entails research of targets' online, network infrastructure studies, information gathered on key members, and privileged access to themselves.

• ***Initial compromise:*** The attacker gains initial access to the network of the targeted organization through known attack vectors and sophisticated social engineering techniques, which may include spear phishing emails, or by taking advantage of any known software vulnerability. This stage is the root of the subsequent attack stages.

• ***Establishing a foot hold:*** Once the attacker gains access inside the target network, he or she then proceeds to establish a persistent and covert presence: custom-built malware is installed with hidden backdoors, allowing him or her to maintain long-term access and control of the compromised systems even if security measures and incident responses are implemented.

• ***Side-to-side movement:*** From the originally compromised point, the attacker simply moves laterally through the target's network to access more systems and data repositories. With advanced techniques that help him evade detection, the attacker continues his lateral movement without making the operation any noisier than it needed to be.

- ***Data exfiltration:*** The end objective behind an APT attack includes the systematic and surreptitious extraction of sensitive data, like IPs, financial records, or government secret information. The attacker will typically use encryption channels or covert communication to export the extracted information without being detected.

3.3.2 Defending Against Advanced Persistent Threats: A Multifaceted Approach

Advanced Persistent Threats are challenging, sophisticated, and relentless threats in that they cannot be defended against using just one defensive layer. One would need several defensive layers, such as proactive ones, for a multidimensional, resiliency-built, and intelligent security strategy aimed at countering this complex type of advanced cyber threat and attack. Therefore, robust defense needs the organizations to work on advanced threat intelligence, robust vulnerability management, intensive network security monitoring, strong endpoint security, and security awareness education of their staff. With this overall security framework in place, an organization will significantly improve its chances of preventing, detecting, and responding to persistent and evasive tactics from APT actors as they try to steal sensitive information, sabotage its critical assets, and erode its overall operational resilience.

- ***Threat intelligence:*** This calls for continued vigilance over the latest APT activity, attack patterns, and indicators of compromise. Thus, monitoring and analyzing threat intelligence helps organizations become better equipped at detecting and responding to attacks early in their stages of occurrence, where they cannot do major damage.

- ***Vulnerability management:*** Vulnerabilities on the software used are identified at regular intervals along with their prioritizations and patching. Strong configurations in security mechanisms along with upgrading systems reduce this attack surface extensively, limiting options for APT actors to exploit for initial access.

- ***Network security:*** This monitoring is also essential because deploying full network security monitoring tools and solutions helps to catch the suspicious activity or even possible APT intrusion attempts. Organizations may continuously monitor, analyze, and detect threats that could be rapidly identified and mitigated by any malicious activity.

- ***Strong protection at the endpoints:*** One more strategic layer of security for APT is endpoint defense. The practice involves the provision of strong anti-virus softwares, solutions to endpoint detection and response together with data-loss prevention tools; thus, detecting, preventing as well as halting APT activity on computers.

- ***Security awareness training:*** Educate and empower your employees to recognize the threats from APTs in terms of which are the commonly used tactics found in social engineering attacks such as phishing; hence, one of the major steps before any initial compromise can be launched into the formation of these very advanced campaigns.

On the other hand, if the multifaceted security strategy that includes all these aspects is implemented, then such organizations will be in a better position to protect critical assets and infrastructure from Advanced Persistent Threats. Advanced Persistent Threats are the ever-evolving serious threats that put organizations and governments in all parts of the world at grave risk. Highly sophisticated, targeted, and resourceful cyberattacks can lead to devastating effects that range from stealing sensitive data and intellectual property to disrupting critical infrastructures. It, therefore, demands a comprehensive and multi-layered security strategy within an organization. This includes good threat intelligence, proactive management of vulnerabilities, sophisticated network monitoring, endpoint security measures, and above all, employee training on how to be responsible and safe. The vigilant and continually improving posture, with a resilient approach, is one of the best ways in which organizations can defend themselves against APT actors and their persistent and evasive tactics. The lack of this might bring severe and long-term consequences, which means that having a strong security framework is of great importance to any organization interested in safeguarding its critical assets and ensuring operational resilience against such advanced cyber threats.

3.4 Phishing Attacks

Phishing attacks have emerged as sophisticated, deceptive attacks on the identity and security mechanisms, where maladjusted actors attempt to impersonate trustworthy organizations or people to exploit their victims. It is based on highly persuasive fraudulent emails or websites or other types of communication such as texts that appear legal but create fear or a time urgency that provokes the uninformed victim to react immediately to it. Attackers lure users to enter their usernames, passwords, financial details, or other personal information to get unauthorized access to accounts, start fraudulent transactions, and even help with malware infections or identity theft. Phishing attacks have many serious effects for victims, who might face huge financial losses, damaged credit scores, and long procedures for identity theft recovery. Moreover, attackers may use compromised accounts and personal data for further malicious activities against the victim and his or her acquaintances, who are constantly being threatened. Psychological consequences of these phishing attacks may also be high because the victims might experience violation, feelings of guilt, and lose their trust in digital systems and services. In essence, it would be important in mitigating purposes in the impacts created by the phishing attacks while using layers of the well-developed robust security and adequate education plus vigilance on verifying forms for suspicious communications or requests regarding sensitive data.

3.4.1 How Do Phishing Attacks Work?

Phishing attacks ruthlessly work on human psychology and interpersonal trust. Crafting convincing messages, an attacker creates the urgency or fears of a subject to prompt them for an immediate reply without much critical analysis involved. Such scams usually have web links to deceptive websites, which almost resemble authentic pages to log on or submit application forms. By falling for those tactics, unsuspecting victims unconsciously hand out their sensitive credentials directly to malicious actors, laying themselves open for further exploitation in the form of possible identity thefts, financial losses, and further devastating effects. Most phishing attacks make use of various arsenals in tricking and influencing the victim. Among these common techniques, phishing messages pretend to be emails coming from big known organizations. They may come out so convincingly professional in the appearance of their logos, branding, and wording. Such phishing emails can falsely indicate problems with one's account, demand security updates that must be performed immediately, or even provide exciting offers with an intent to provoke a response with sensitive information.

Another common practice is the generation of phishing websites that are designed to look like original online services. These phishing websites can be very identical to their actual counterparts, but with slight differences in the URL or design. Whenever a victim tries to access his or her accounts on these fraudulent websites, their usernames, passwords, financial details, and many other pieces of personal information can be seized and used for malicious purposes by the attackers who launched the attack. Phishing threats are not limited to email; attackers use this as a medium to text (smishing) and call (vishing) as well to reach their victims. Smishing contains attacks where an attacker uses the texts to incite the victim to click on the malicious links or share sensitive information as it often comes with package deliveries, bank alerts, or other such significant matters. Vishing, however, is when the perpetrator acts like a reputable institution, like a bank or a government office, and pressures the victim into giving away private information over the phone. Such various phishing methods have demonstrated the resourcefulness and ability of cyberthieves to take advantage of human psychology and social trust for nefarious purposes. Phishing attacks are, thus, ever-changing and represent an ongoing and present threat, where vigilance, education of the user, and strong security can be considered essential to reduce their impact.

3.4.2 Protecting Against Phishing Attacks

This calls for protection against phishing in a way that involves multiple components: the security culture, adequate education for the users, and technical security. These must involve email filtering powered by machine learning and threat intelligence as well as the anti-phishing software used for the detection of suspicious websites and links to give users the alarm, alongside conducting frequent user training and awareness programs in an attempt to enable them to identify these deception tactics. This would also mean adding security by enabling multi-factor authentication for critical accounts and systems, which would make it well-nigh impossible to gain unauthorized access, even with login credentials obtained through a successful phishing attack.

(a) Email filtering: Using advanced email filtering that is powered by machine learning and threat intelligence helps significantly block the number of phishing emails reaching users' inboxes. Using such powerful filters that check and scrutinize all ranges of characteristics, from sender authenticity, message content, and embedded links, it is able to minutely detect and quarantine any suspicious messages that pose a potential threat. With the support of the advanced innovations in AI and real-time threat intelligence, such email filter systems can flag even the most complex phishing attacks way ahead of impact and help make an important early defense against these constantly growing types of cybersecurity attacks.

(b) Anti-phishing Software: Dedicated anti-phishing software installed on corporate and personal devices can be provided to defend against phishing attacks. They make use of a live threat database and heuristic analysis in order to detect and warn the user about suspicious websites and links from reaching a particular phishing site, where they could inadvertently disclose sensitive information. Anti-phishing software can effectively warn users of a threat by monitoring known phishing sites and recognizing the patterns of fraudulent behavior. Through this, they can make proper decisions and avoid such malicious attempts at stealing their data or compromising their accounts.

(c) User education: This is educating a user on possible phishing attacks and related warning signs, including comprehensive training on how to distinguish phishing attempts—for example, identifying suspicious sources of emails and verifying the actual authenticity of websites, as well as keeping away from solicitations for personal information or financial credentials. Regular awareness campaigns, interactive workshops, and simulated phishing exercises should be implemented as a way to foster a security culture in any organization.

Through this, users will be prepared to actively participate in defending their organization against deceptive threats. Such preparedness ensures that users are more knowledgeable and competent in identifying phishing attempts and staying away from such attacks, therefore strengthening the cybersecurity posture of organizations and minimizing attacks that exploit vulnerabilities in humans.

(d) Multi-factor authentication: For all critical accounts and systems, enable multi-factor authentication. That will add one more layer of security, meaning it will become much harder for attackers to log in even when they have successful phishing attacks where they obtain the login credentials. In the case of MFA, there is a secondary step required from the users for verification-possibly through their mobile device for a one-time code, fingerprint or facial recognition biometric, or even through a hardware security key. Adding one more step between a simple login with username and password provides a better hindrance to unwanted actors and creates a greater reduction in the account compromise even though an attacker should steal the user's main login credentials.

The simplest way for organizations to prevent devastating consequences posed by phishing attacks is by applying a holistic defense-in-depth approach that implements proactive user education and advanced technical controls. The possibility of defense against these emerging threats is created via layered security, and this includes robust email filtering, anti-phishing software, and updated user education, all aimed at robustness in defense. Phishing attacks are a very common and constantly evolving threat in the digital world. With cybercriminals constantly changing their tactics, it is essential for individuals and organizations to be updated on the latest phishing techniques and take the right security measures to be better protected against these fraudulent attacks. Through vigilance and a robust security framework, users and organizations can strengthen their resilience and protect their sensitive information against the constant and widespread risk of phishing.

3.5 Zero-Day Exploits

Zero-day exploits are a very dangerous weapon in the toolkit of a cyber attacker. They represent software vulnerabilities as to which the author or developer would not be knowledgeable, meaning they have no solution when attacks occur. Consequently, this so-called "zero-day" gap in vulnerability finds systems without defensive capabilities, in which the wrongdoer enjoys the opportunity before the developers come up with remedies. A successful zero-day exploit can lead to catastrophic consequences, including data breaches and system compromise, ransomware attacks, and wide-scale disruption. Zero-day exploits are extremely valuable to cybercriminals and nation-state actors because they can bypass traditional security measures and gain unauthorized access to sensitive systems and data. Without any available remedy, there is an unfortunate vulnerability on the part of an organization or individuals to devastating impact from zero-day attacks that range from financial and reputational costs to operational damage.

Zero-day exploits are highly valuable to cybercriminals and nation-state actors because of the effectiveness and stealth of these exploits. They are difficult to detect with traditional solutions, as the goal for traditional solutions is to provide detection based on signatures or patterns generated from known malware or attacks. The discovery and development of zero-day exploits require technical expertise and a lot of resources, such as reverse engineering software, code analysis for vulnerabilities, and individually designing custom exploit code. These are exploits from research and analysis painstakingly done on security researchers or even malicious actors. It may identify flaws that no one else ever noticed in a piece of software or system, studying source codes, memory usage, and possibly running through numerous execution paths looking for weaknesses that no one had time to fix from the side of the vendors. This makes attackers have an advantage because their activities cannot be detected or prevented using traditional security measures. The development of zero-day exploits usually requires a high understanding of the architecture of the targeted software, programming languages, and security mechanisms, making them very valuable and highly sought after in the world of cyber threats.

The lifecycle of a zero-day exploit basically consists of three distinct and vital stages:

- ***Discovery:*** An unknown, previously undisclosed, and unpatched software vulnerability is slowly discovered through meticulous efforts of a highly advanced security researcher or by a sophisticated hacker or an accident serendipitously. This was a significant breakthrough as it exposed a design or implementation weakness in the software that had avoided the attention of the vendor as well as the general cybersecurity world.

- ***Development:*** The exploitation is highly crafted to completely leverage the newly discovered vulnerability. The process requires great analysis on software architecture, extreme reverse engineering, and designing unique, technically intense code capable of consistently invoking the vulnerability while initiating malicious operations. A zero-day exploit takes serious programming languages and memory management know-how in tandem with an in-depth knowledge of security mechanisms.

- ***Weaponization:*** The developed exploit is then weaponized within malware or sophisticated attack tools. It becomes a highly potent and silent weapon for the cybercriminals or nation-state actors. In weaponization, the exploit is integrated into the broader attack framework or malicious payload to ensure it can be successfully launched against the target systems.

• ***Deployment:*** This is the armed exploitation of the zero-day, deployed against the victim, using sophisticatedly created phishing emails or malicious websites, stealthy attack vectors, and even through social engineering attacks that may avoid security controls. The moment for the attack is crucial; zero-day exploits are disclosed, and patches could be released anytime.

• ***Disclosure/Patching:*** Sooner or later, the flaw is disclosed to the software's vendor, and the latter seriously engages in developing an update or a patch to remove the flaw so that the attackers' "window of opportunity" is closed within the "zero-day" vulnerability. This might be done either by the originator of the security research or through a responsible disclosure program; even the miscreants who discovered the exploit may sell the exploit on the black market or hold it in reserve for possible later use.

3.5.1 Mitigation of Zero-Day Exploits

To protect against zero-day exploits, a proactive approach, in which different strategies and technologies are combined with multi-layered security, is needed.

(1) Threat intelligence: It is very important to be aware of the latest threat landscape and the potential zero-day vulnerabilities. Organizations should monitor the security bulletins closely, subscribe to the best possible threat intelligence services, and engage in the close cooperation of security researchers and related communities in the industry to stay ahead of emerging threats. Such a thorough awareness of the threat environment helps organizations prepare and respond accordingly to zero-day attacks.

(2) Vulnerability management: All vulnerability management in place basically means scanning systems all the time for vulnerabilities, prioritizing quickly patching the most serious security flaws, and applying security updates when necessary. During this process, the constant surveillance and remediation of vulnerabilities will help decrease the footprint of an attack and lower the impact of a zero-day exploit before it becomes successful.

(3) Intrusion detection and prevention system: Advanced systems for intrusion detection and prevention, which may have the capability of detecting and preventing suspicious activity, even without matching known signatures of attacks, can be effective. These systems observe network traffic as well as the behavior of the system for continuous monitoring to identify anomalies indicative of a zero-day attack using techniques such as machine learning and behavioral analysis. Immediate detection and response to such a threat may thus be important for limiting the spread of zero-day exploits.

(4) Sandboxing: Additional protection from zero-day exploits—Sandboxing employs sandboxing technologies, where questionable files or apps are run safely in an isolated environment, thereby ensuring the organization conducts its analysis without compromising the company's critical productions. It allows no execution of malicious code within the system or any risk exposure.

(5) Security awareness and training: Educating employees to recognize potential threats and make them empowered and vigilant is very important in security strategy. As awareness of what not to do, such as clicking on suspicious links or opening attachments from unknown parties, can protect against the very first compromise and prevent the full exploitation of the zero-day, empowered and vigilant employees can substantially reduce the attack surface and the overall security posture.

Implementing a multi-layered approach to security should be fundamental in the efforts made by an organization to effectively prepare, detect, and respond to the persistent and continually evolving zero-day exploits threat. These are amongst the vulnerabilities causing significant challenges, which, indeed, are ever-present, challenging cybersecurity measures that can be unearthed and armed by such sharp adversaries so stealthy, devastating attacks can be perpetrated. With a proactive security posture and robust defense mechanisms, organizations can better protect themselves from these dangerous and unpredictable threats. This holistic approach relies on threat intelligence to be ahead of emerging vulnerabilities, uses advanced vulnerability management to identify and remediate critical issues as soon as possible, has advanced intrusion detection and prevention systems to monitor anomalous activity, uses sandboxing technology to analyze and contain suspect files in a safe environment, and provides security awareness training that empowers the employees to know and report suspected threats. Collectively, the multifaceted security controls are important as they help control the impact of zero-day exploits and protect all critical systems, networks, and data from this elusive and potentially potent cyber threat.

3.6 Insider Threats

Insider threats are among the most significant and complex risks to the security of any organization. These threats stem from insiders who were assigned official authorization to access sensitive information or systems but have since misused the same in an intentional or reckless manner. These malicious or careless individuals can be either present or former employees, contractors, or other business partners with whom they maintain a special relationship. The impact of insider threats can be devastating, from breach of data and loss in finances to loss in reputation and operational standards. Insider threats are concerning because the person involved is already well-acquainted with the systems, processes, and weaknesses of the organization. Such insiders can exploit that knowledge to deliver significant damage to the organization that is not always easy to discover and correct. Malicious insiders may be financially motivated, have personal scores to settle, or be driven by ideological convictions. Negligent insiders compromise security through lack of care or information. Malicious activities can be carried out within the organization from compromised insiders who have accounts or credentials hijacked by external attackers.

Counter-strategy to an insider threat challenge must be comprehensive and multi-layered, exercising robust access controls, rigor in monitoring and auditing, effective data loss prevention, broad security awareness training of employees, and even a comprehensive background check on personnel who are trusted with sensitive information or systems. Only through the adoption of a proactively holistic security posture can an organization hope to significantly mitigate the grave and perpetual threat from inside its pillars caused by those who abuse their privileged access.

3.6.1 Types of Insider Threats

Insider threats can be categorized into several distinct types:

(i) Malicious insiders: These actors, with their complex mix of motivations, abuse their privileged access to sensitive information or systems for malicious purposes. They can be motivated by greed for money as they seek to sell valuable data or intellectual property for financial gain. Others have an intense sense of resentment or a need to get revenge against an organization that they believe has wronged them or done them an injustice. In addition, other malicious insiders are driven by ideological beliefs or extremist views and do so to cause intentional damage to the security and interests of the organization as they pursue what they believe to be their political or social cause. Nonetheless, whatever the cause may be, these malicious actors will cause significant damage as they use the very close familiarity they have with the organization's systems and vulnerabilities. Negligent insiders inadvertently compromise organizational security due to ignorance, recklessness, lack of security awareness, and proper security education, which makes them create some loopholes that further put the organization at potential huge risk by indulging in various ways, like becoming easy victims for phishing, using weak passwords and repeated usages of previous ones, and poor storage and disposal practices for confidential documents. Without an appropriate understanding of best practices for cybersecurity and potential long-term consequences of their actions, negligent insiders are an easy target for exploitation, thereby compromising the critical systems, networks, and data of an organization. One needs a strong security culture, with employees given proper information and empowered to manage the organization's security posture and held accountable.

(ii) Compromised insiders: Compromised insiders refer to users who have their account or credentials stolen by an attacker from outside and whose access is subsequently used by that attacker to commit malicious activities quietly from within the organization in which they had been entrusted. This is an insidious and very challenging threat since the malicious activity seems to originate from a valid, authorized source within the organization, thereby becoming very difficult to detect and to effectively mitigate. The inside entity with intimate knowledge of the systems, processes, and vulnerabilities in the organization thus enables the attackers outside the organization to breach its defenses and possibly exploit its internal vulnerabilities without creating any apparent alarms. This form of insider threat is especially troublesome because it might allow the adversaries to carry out their malicious aims undetected, thus leaving havoc on critical assets, operations, and reputations within an organization.

3.6.2 Motivations and Indicators

Awareness of various motivations behind the insider threat requires proper understanding before devising proper mitigation strategies. Common motivations may include:

- ***Financial gain:*** This type of threat can be primarily motivated by financial gains for a personal enrichment scheme, like theft and sale of sensitive data or intellectual property to earn money. This could include theft and sale to the highest bidder of valuable customer information, trade secrets, or other confidential data through illicit channels. The significant monetary gain at stake can be an incentive for the malicious insider who wants to take advantage of the authorized access with which he is entrusted and exploit the trust put in him by the organization.

- ***Revenge:*** Ingrained disgruntled employees or others who feel that they are treated unfairly may wish to hurt the organization in terms of revenge. Such malcontents can leak corporate secrets, get involved in critical operations disruption, or even sabotage some systems for what is perceived as corporate mis-treatment. These malicious insiders are usually motivated by a personal vendetta against the organization.

- ***Ideological beliefs:*** Insider threats may also arise from deep-rooted political or ideological convictions and a desire to undermine the organization's interests or further personal agendas. They will leak sensitive information or even want to cause organizational disruption due to a perceived legitimacy of their acts in pursuit of a higher purpose or a higher good in which they believe, or a good that their conscience and personal philosophy dictate as good.

It is through this understanding of the multifaceted motives of money, personal vengeance, and even ideological extremism that a strategic countermeasure approach can be developed within the organization to foster a security-conscious culture. With more understanding in this domain of complex and multifaceted motivations behind insider threats, organizations can, in turn, prepare more for the detection of these serious risks and build more robust resilience in dealing with their critical assets.

Indicators of potential insider threats can include:

(a) Suspicious access patterns: Access outside of normal times, from unidentified locations, at odd hours, or anything else that resembles a pattern as if the personnel are trying to move data out might be a sure indicator of the presence of a malicious insider attack. This deviation in access from normal times means that the accessing personnel are operating undercover, probably to extract highly sensitive information of some sort—mostly for fraudulent purposes, maybe revenge, or perhaps ideological. This could be a signal that the employee is intentionally trying to evade being caught while pursuing unauthorized activities because his normal access patterns are different. It is through close monitoring and investigation of such deviations in access patterns that serious risks may be identified and mitigated by counteracting insider threats. These very subtle behavioral cues from an individual may offer excellent insight into what that individual might look to compromise or exfiltrate systems and data.

(b) Large-scale data transfers: There should be a high likelihood to flag significant suspicion with major and immediate investigation where employees copy or transfer vast amounts of data, such as a few gigabytes or terabytes, to outside devices, cloud storage platforms, or other unauthorized destinations. This behavior could indicate a malicious insider's intentional attempt to steal or exfiltrate sensitive, proprietary, or confidential information for personal gain or to share with unauthorized third parties. These may actually surpass usual file sizes and use patterns in their scale and volume and would probably reflect an intentional attempt at retrieving valuable intellectual property, trade secrets, customer data, or other key assets for purposes such as financial gains, competitive advantages, or ideologic causes. This way, monitoring in detail these very large-scale information transfers along with other behavioral trends is critical and helps in the timely identification and alleviation of inside threats trying to compromise the organizations' most valuable.

(c) Behavioral changes: Sudden, undiagnosed changes in the behavior of an employee-a high level of stress, financial problems, overt disgruntlement, or mood swings-would be some indicator of personal or professional issues that could feed into the creation of insider threats. Such behavioral indicators, once noticed, are to be closely monitored and investigated to pinpoint the causes and repercussions on security. Significant life events, job-related stressors, or changes in employees' financial or mental well-being can make them feel the urge to take drastic actions, even to the point of betraying the trust the organization has vested in them. Therefore, careful consideration and examination of behavioral changes from insider actors offer useful organizational knowledge concerning potentially discontent or unfaithful insiders to react towards those dangers even before these deteriorate into adverse security breach activities or worse misbehavior.

Mitigating such a dynamically fluctuating problem in the form of an insider attack necessitates using the multi-layered and fully integrated nature of security as mitigation. Notably, those major strategies underlie the ability as follows:

- ***Control access:*** Providing firm access-control mechanisms based upon a principle, such as that for 'least access, least need-to-know, or more simply, "need-only" permits giving a damaging attacker only whatever information and level he or she will need. This minimizes the exploitation of authorized access to sensitive information or mission-critical systems for nefarious purposes.

- ***Monitoring and auditing:*** Through frequent monitoring of user activities and detailed auditing of system logs, suspect behavioral patterns, such as unusual access of sensitive data or large-scale data transfer, are more likely to be detected for an early warning system to prompt intervention. That way, through proactive means, insider threats can be identified and dealt with before they escalate into a damaging security breach.

- ***Data loss prevention:*** Sensitive data will leave an organization only with the implementation of advanced data loss prevention tools and technologies because the enforcement is as strict. Although malicious insiders had a means of accessing and exfiltrating critical information and trade secrets or intellectual property, it became significantly difficult. Organizations can better hold on to critical assets through DLP solutions.

- ***Security awareness training:*** This ensures educating and equipping employees regarding potential insider threats, including threat and indicator-related aspects, besides preparing them for awareness on suspecting and reporting suspect activities to effectively promote an active, security-minded culture inside the organization, providing the necessary capabilities for more additional layers of protection against the potential insider threat.

- ***Background checks and ongoing monitoring:*** Thorough pre-employment background checks as well as subsequent personnel screening through active monitoring will better identify the vulnerabilities and issues for access to critical information or missions. This allows the organization a continued sense of vigilance for insider threats to be detected or prevented by its employees' ongoing behavior monitored, constantly evaluated, or reviewed.

Combining these with a broad and multi-layer approach through solid technical controls, thorough monitoring, and audit together with awareness security training and initiatives, insider threats are well poised to dramatically up the overall levels of resilience on the part of an organization as it responds and prepares for this challenging, evolving context. Therefore, the approach, being holistic in this case by addressing human and technological aspects to effectively identify the myriads of different risks presented with malicious insiders when attempting to acquire an organization's sensitive information or its critical or mission-critical assets/systems, is paramount in managing them all. Technical controls like the principle of least privilege may limit the malicious insider's potential damage by allowing access to only the systems and data needed. Continuous monitoring and auditing of user activity will be able to help detect suspicious behavioral patterns in time to ensure early detection and prompt intervention before the security breach escalates. Additionally, data-loss prevention tools and technologies are better suited to protecting sensitive information such that no possibility exists for leaking sensitive information within or out from the organization for malicious insiders wishing to exfiltrate valuable information, secrets, or IPs. In addition to these technical countermeasures, there is also the human element involved in addressing insider threats. Through security awareness training, the organization empowers employees to be more aware of and to report suspicious activities, hence providing a solid security-conscious culture in the organization. Thorough pre-employment background checks and continued personnel screening will also identify possible risks and concerns before giving them access to sensitive information or critical systems for a mission.

The challenge that insider threats pose to an organization is quite complex and changing. Organizations are, therefore, able to defend themselves against the devastating effects of insider attacks if they implement a holistic security strategy that addresses technical and human factors.

4 An Improved Logo-Based Phishing Detection System

Abstract: Phishing attacks continue to be a major cybersecurity threat, exploiting users through deceptive websites that mimic legitimate entities. This paper presents an improved logo-based phishing detection system that enhances accuracy in identifying fraudulent websites. The study reviews existing phishing detection techniques, highlighting their limitations and the need for more robust solutions. The proposed methodology leverages advanced image processing and machine learning classifier models to detect manipulated logos and flag potential phishing attempts. Experimental results demonstrate the system's effectiveness in distinguishing genuine and malicious sites with higher precision compared to existing methods. This research contributes to the development of stronger anti-phishing mechanisms, improving online security and user protection.

Keywords: Phishing detection, Logo-based authentication, Machine learning, Cybersecurity, Image processing

4.1 Introduction

In the modern era of computation, cyber-physical systems (CPSs) have become the backbone of the Internet, which works seamlessly and integrates with the computational and physical domains. The CPS that merge computational and physical processes are a fundamental aspect of future Internet infrastructure. Nevertheless, these modern systems are also responsible for producing more complex forms of cyberattacks. Traditional security solutions applied in real-time with advancements work edge-to-edge to meet protocols and regulations of the cyber systems, and they even struggle to meet the demands of real-time traffic and secure the cyber-physical system simultaneously.

The most common form of cyber threat is phishing. With the advanced tools of web design, the phishing attack is more precise and accurate to convince the victim. The recent forms of phishing attacks are mostly hybrid ones, such as web phishing combined with phone phishing, which are more successful at producing an authentic image to the victim to fall into the trap. From pretending they are genuine websites to coming up with complex email frauds, the techniques employed in phishing attacks keep advancing, making it hard for cybersecurity professionals to deal with them.

Among the various categories of phishing detection, the logo-based phishing detection is more effective and promising one. This is because the detection mechanism simply looks for a reputed brand logo in the content, which does not belong to the legitimate firm. The techniques utilized are dynamic and visually deceptive, which validates the existence of existing security protocols as being less operative. The gravity of the matter is emphasized by the fact that classical approaches struggle to provide robust protection against these maturing and sophisticated logo-based phishing attacks within the Cyber-Physical Systems.

4.2 Phishing Attacks

People have recently been involved in much bigger online deals, from simple buying and selling to internet banking and bill payments, purchasing a mortgage or automobile loan, and paying tax due. The rise in online transactions has been associated with an increase in online threats. Phishing is a security threat that employs social engineering and spoofs websites to deceive people into revealing their secret data. Phishing attacks are now fairly widespread, and many ways to detect them exist. Often, phishing attacks originate from malevolent links that make victims visit a fake website where they are illegitimately convinced to provide confidential details such as secret codes, passwords, OTPs, financial account data, and security numbers. This collected information was used to perform genuine electronic communications as the victim. Phishing attacks are mostly associated with e-commerce sites, banks' portals, and web pages with personal information. Such phishing tactics often steal things like user login IDs/passwords, credit card numbers, ATM pins, etc. The victim ultimately experiences a substantial financial loss and sometimes defamation.

According to Das et al. [4], a typical phishing attempt consists of three steps: First, the mailer's botnet sends out massive volumes of malicious emails containing enticing subject lines and attachments such as images or links. The user is redirected to the collector's website, which is a fake site with phishers requesting personal login passwords, bank information, and card details. If the user submits the above data, then the cashier uses this collected information to arrive at a payout. Different types of phishing attacks are shown in Figure 4.1.

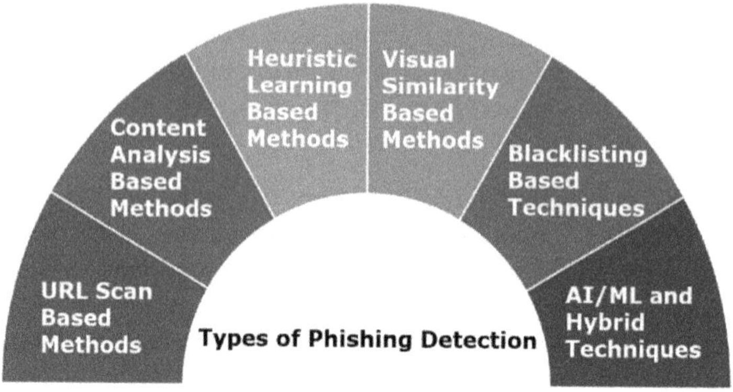

Figure 4.1 Categorization of phishing attack detection

An overview of the category types of phishing detection systems of the Figure 4.1 are described as follows:

(1) URL scans phishing detection: In this technique, different variables of interest are extracted for the suspicious URL, and their pattern is found to identify anomalies associated with phishing sites. This method finds potential URLs by creating different combinatorial URLs from already valid URLs and discovers whether they are associated with phishing history.

(2) Content-based phishing detection: This technique focuses on finding the pattern and anomalies in the content present in the given context (e.g., email, URLs, website). In consideration of this technique, DOM is also evaluated with previous anomalies and signatures of phishing behavior.

(3) Heuristic-learning-based technique: This technique depends upon the better heuristics collected over a period of time and built for the observation of finding anomalies in web apps. Heuristics are used to find abnormal behaviors on suspected websites. Final anomaly detection uses a set of predefined heuristics and the rules derived from assimilation algorithms.

(4) Visual-similarity-based approach: This technique implements the visual similarity scores, which are calculated for the detection of phishing attempts; the calculated score is used in the visual-similarity algorithm to confirm the phishing attempt. Various parameters like logos, pictures, font size, type, alignment, and text position are considered to calculate the score.

(5) Blacklisting techniques: In this approach. A database of domain names, URLs, and phishing discovered in the past is maintained. The method works by comparing the suspected websites and database maintained; this method can be made complex by creating different types of blacklists.

(6) Hybrid approach and artificial intelligence/machine learning (ML): Different supervised learning algorithms with relevant feature extraction are applied to achieve better accuracy in the model built, which can be later integrated into real-world phishing detection systems.

4.3 Literature Survey

Many researchers have come up with different approaches to prevent and detect phishing attacks, but there is a need for precise and accurate methods that can help prevent these attacks.

Mishra et al. [1] have elaborated a method to detect phishing by using the average color of each hue in an image's centroid and the density distribution for that hue as a feature. The goal was to prevent phishing attacks by differentiating authentic logos from fake ones with machine learning algorithms. This paper demonstrates that detecting logo-based phishing requires recognizing specific patterns in pixel distributions related to hues found within images, thus offering new approaches to battling cybercrime involving deception. Varshney et al. [2] have conducted a comprehensive analysis, exploring different ways to detect phished websites. In addition to outlining new methods, they have also examined the limitations and strengths of every technique. Their method has provided a basis for recognizing different phishing detection systems by appraising their merits alongside demerits.

In a meticulous survey, Mishra et al. [3] have focused on detecting phishing in the Internet of Things (IoT)-based Cyber-Physical Human Systems. This paper provides a detailed study of various hybrid forms and combinations of multiple phishing detection techniques. The authors have identified the fact that these techniques require high computational costs. Nevertheless, they have asserted that data mining and ML methods outperform other approaches in terms of accuracy and false positive rates. Das et al. [4] have systematically classified various methods in their comprehensive review of machine-learning-based algorithms for detecting phishing and examined these different methods. This detailed examination has summarized that ML-based algorithms have improved accuracy, albeit with higher computational costs. They provide an interesting comparison between True Positive Rate (TPR) and False Positive Rate (FPR) for many different ML algorithms, which can signal the strengths and weaknesses of using machine learning in phishing detection systems.

Chiew et al. [5] have studied and highlighted the importance of logo image features in the detection of phishing. They have provided an identity consistency verification between genuine and projected websites, using logo images. This work has highlighted that the representation of logos with simple color features can also be used to detect phishing attacks in CPS. For brand detection, Bozkir et al. [6] proposed a method called LogoSENSE, which is based on the Histogram Oriented Gradient (HOG) feature. To make it more useful in the identification of logos that are scale-invariant, this technique uses a Support Vector Machine (SVM) classifier with HOG for phishing webpage detection and logo classification. In their study, Yao et al. [7] have used Faster R-CNN (Region-based Convolutional Neural Network) to detect URL phishing and small logo recognition. Their DL method is important in identifying two-dimensional and small-scale logos specifically for code-based attacks. In their research, Lin et al. [8], Phishpedia is introduced as a system that uses a DL model. Its main aims include finding similar logo variations and identifying identity logos in order to detect phishing attempts. Despite its promising accuracy, the proposed work has smaller yet considerable cases of false detection.

Wang et al. [9] have used computer vision algorithms to identify phishing attacks. Their algorithm confirms a phishing attack by asking questions and eliminates the false positive cases by filtering the keyboard entries. Their visual approach of combining interactive elements with computer-vision algorithms provides a practical way of detecting phishing that takes into account both the visual and interactive nature thereof. Rao et al. [10] have proposed a technique, Jail-Phish, to improve the capability of search engine-based strategies in identifying newly registered genuine websites and phishing websites hosted on compromised servers (PSHCS). This method verifies the accuracy of its results by calculating similarity scores, especially logo similarities. In order to detect phishing websites more accurately, this algorithm employs a refined heuristic technique that uses search engine-based methods and logo similarities at the same time.

Peng et al. [11] have put forward a Natural Language Processing (NLP)-based approach for identifying phishing statements in a given text. Their method is centered around the use of NLP with ML to detect different variants of phishing attacks. Azeez et al. [12] have contributed a method of whitelisting to detect phishing attacks that can be automated by comparing IP addresses and domain names. The known popular sites are compared with visually analyzed links through the use of a procedure that then draws conclusions based on these similarities. According to them, there is improvement in detection accuracy when visual link comparison is combined with the domain name and IP address analysis. Basit et al. [13] have used the Ensemble Method that combines the Random Forest Classifier with ML classifiers as Artificial Neural Networks (ANN), Decision Trees, and K-Nearest Neighbors (KNN). According to the authors, the Ensemble approach has outperformed all other works. Ruofan et al. [14] have proposed PhishIntention, which is designed to detect phishing intention from webpages through visual brand intention extraction. PhishIntention adds an additional layer that scans through the abstraction of webpage layouts and decouples visual brand identity to identify phishing intent.

From the above study, the following key points are identified:

(i) The ML approaches have better accuracy and are more effective in phishing detection.

(ii) However, ML approaches required a number of steps to preprocess the phishing datasets to make them ready for training.

(iii) Visually similar-based approaches are the most common way to identify a phishing site with greater accuracy.

(iv) The DL models are the future of ML, and compared to the ML techniques, the DL models are better with image data.

The fake or real logo detection process is described in Figure 4.2.

4.4 Proposed Methodology

In this section, we discuss the proposed deep learning models to detect logos of popular phishing brands. Figure 4.2 demonstrates the high-level architecture of the fake/real logo detection process. Each phase of the proposed method is described in the following sections.

4.4.1 Data Acquisition & Preprocessing

Dataset: The dataset consists of the newest logos of some top phishing brands in South Asia. The dataset is made up of train and test folders that also contain subfolders for fake and genuine images of each logo.

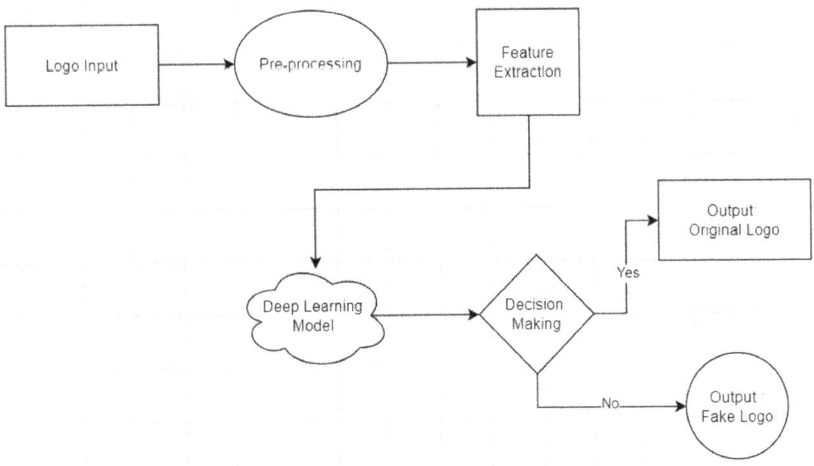

Figure 4.2 Design flow of fake/real logo detection

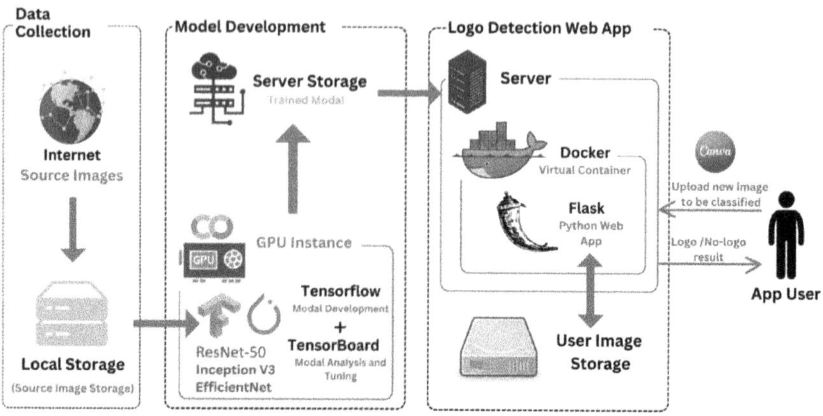

Figure 4.3 Work flow for logo detection

Logo Extraction: Legitimate corporate logos were acquired from the websites of businesses, while counterfeit ones were gathered through phishing reports variously. The images of trademarks were manipulated by rotating them and adjusting their RGB and grayscale representations a little bit by hand to form the fake pictures.

Resizing: The aspect ratio of an image is adjusted to make it be in line with standard measurements. In this case, resizing becomes necessary for uniform dimensions of all the images in a dataset that have to be fed into a neural network model for logo detection. Resizing mostly involves scaling to a suitable size for the input layer of a neural network.

Normalization: Normalization is the term for adjusting pixel values in an image to a standard range. For example, digital images are often represented as integers for each channel (red, green, blue) with values ranging from 0 to 255. The task of normalization in this case involves converting these pixel values into a range—usually between 0 and 1 or −1 and 1—that is more appropriate for training neural networks. Normalization guarantees that the average value of input data tends to be zero while its standard deviation tends towards one, thus improving stability and speeding up training processes.

Figure 4.3 describes the workflow of the logo detection mechanism. It has three phases, namely data collection, model development, and logo detection web app.

4.4.2 Feature Extraction with DL Models

4.4.2.1 Pretrained Convolutional Neural Networks

As shown in Figure 3, three different pre-trained CNN models were implemented to build the objective model. These models are ResNet50, Inception v3, and

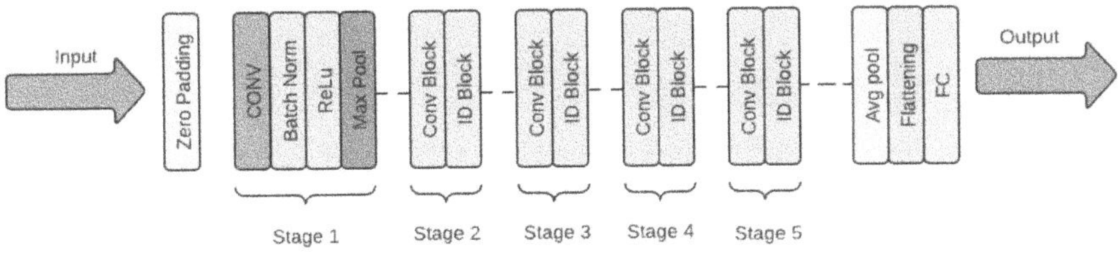

Figure 4.4 ResNet50 Architecture overview

EfficientNet. The models used are previously trained during model building on large-scale image datasets. In this research, those NNs were thoughtfully chosen based on several parameters to address the research objectives efficiently.

1. ResNet50

ResNet50 is chosen due to its fame in image classification tasks. The vanishing gradient issue is circumvented by skip connections and deep architectures, thus enhancing the efficiency of training deep networks. Feature hierarchy at various levels is crucial for detecting logos; this enables recognition of complicated patterns within the images that contain them. Despite being a very advanced model, ResNet50 is still a good trade-off between accuracy and computational efficiency, making it suitable for practical integration into Cyber-Physical Systems (CPS).

A summary of the pre-trained ResNet50 neural network is displayed in Figure 4.4. Microsoft Research created the deep convolutional neural network (CNN) model referred to as ResNet50 in 2015. It is a version of the famous "Residual Network" or simply ResNet architecture. The name ResNet50 comes from its depth, which is 50 layers. The four main parts of the ResNet50 architecture are identity blocks, convolutional, fully connected, and connection layers. The features of the input image captured by CNN are processed and converted by both the identity and convolutional blocks. Fully linked layers are eventually used to determine the final classification.

2. Inception v3

The rationale for using Inception v3 is that its inception modules ease the extraction of features at different scales within a single convolutional layer. The ability to process multiple-scale data is essential for spotting variations of logos of various sizes and complexity levels. This model can be the most appropriate in situations with resource constraints, as in CPS contexts, since it employs depth-wise separable convolutions, which reduce computational complexity without affecting performance. In cases requiring fine-grained feature extraction, such as logo detection in phishing photos, Inception v3

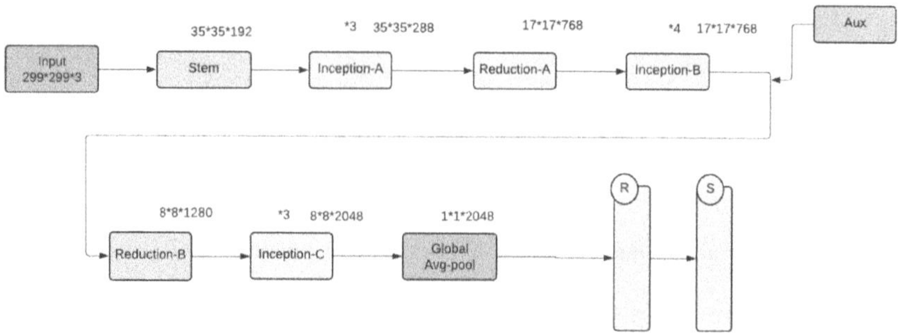

Figure 4.5 Inception V3 Architecture overview

would be a good choice, considering its strong performance on image recognition benchmarks.

As shown in Figure 4.5, the main architecture of InceptionV3. The inception V1 model has been refined and enhanced to create the V3. The Inception V3 model used a number of techniques to optimize the network and enhance model adaptation. It works better. It maintains performance even with a deeper network than the Inception V1 and V2 models. Computing-wise, it is less expensive. It uses auxiliary classifiers as regularizers.

The Inception v3 model, which was released in 2015, has 42 layers total and a lower error rate than its predecessors. Various optimizations were done to improve the Inception V3 model. The principal adjustments done to the Inception V3 model include partitioning into more minimal convolutions, factorization of spatial data into asymmetric convolutions, the use of supplementary classifiers, and effective grid size diminution.

3. EfficientNet

EfficientNet was selected as one of the models because it provides a better efficiency-accuracy trade-off than traditional CNNs. By scaling compound techniques used in the EfficientNet model, designers can come up with models that are more efficient in terms of performance and have fewer parameters. This design supports quick deployment in CPS since these systems might have limited computing resources due to its low computation requirements and parameter-efficient structure of EfficientNet. This project aims to develop an exact logo-based phishing detection system that uses minimal resources. The goal aligns with EfficientNet's requirement for high accuracy and low computation.

The EfficientNet's architecture design is shown in Figure 4.6. In EfficientNet, MBConv layers are comprised of depth-wise separable convolutions and inverted residual blocks. Further, squeeze-and-excitation (SE) optimization

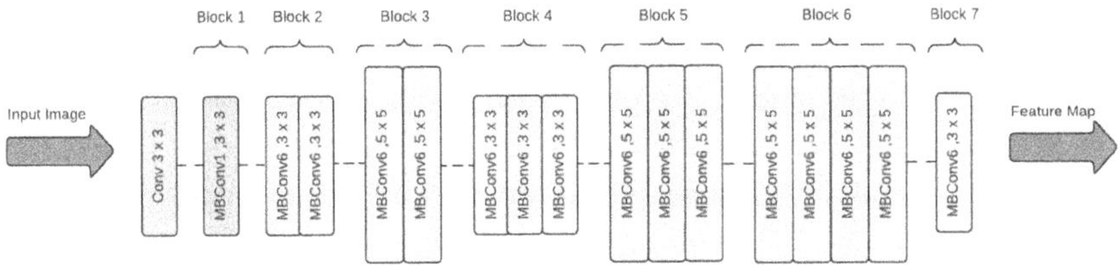

Figure 4.6 EfficientNet Architecture overview

has been incorporated into the model design to improve its performance. For example, the MBConv layer in EfficientNet is so important to its structure. However, it borrows heavily from MobileNetV2's inverted residual blocks with minor tweaks. The combination of these findings led us to develop EfficientNet, a compound scaling method that helps balance between accuracy and efficiency in deep learning. It also offers customizable models through its intelligent width, depth, and resolution scaling for various hardware configurations. Thus, this computer vision workload exhibits excellent performance under squeeze-and-excitation optimization, mobile inverted bottleneck layers, and robust, lightweight architecture.

By leveraging these diverse deep learning architectures, our research aims to explore the effectiveness of different models in the context of logo-based phishing detection in Cyber-Physical Systems. The selection of ResNet50, Inception v3, and EfficientNet was driven by their architectural characteristics, computational efficiency, and demonstrated performance in similar image recognition tasks. By empirical evaluation, we want to determine which model or group of models is most appropriate for use in the real world, with consideration of factors like scalability, computational cost, and accuracy in CPS situations.

4.4.3 Fine-tuning

Using the pre-trained CNN model for feature extraction, fine-tuning is needed on the model to make logo classification work effectively. Adjusting the parameters for pre-trained models according to the logo detection dataset needs to be done for model fine-tuning. Disclosing the models to the dataset in the time of fine-tuning provides the model flexibility so that it can learn to extract features that are pertinent for differentiating among and between the various logos. This procedure promotes an upgrade of the achievement of the models on the varied tasks while using the notion capabilities learned during pretraining.

4.5 Classifier Models

In the phishing logo classifier phase, a neural network model was designed to identify logos. The training of the classifier from scratch is done to make the classifier learn the difference between genuine and false logos. Each logo image contained in the dataset has mapping with its associated label, which gives proof of its trueness. The gradient-based learning relies on the use of algorithms in training to enable the neural network to learn how to associate input logo images with their corresponding labels. The proposed classifier identifies a logo by considering a series of features such as color transitions, texture design, and geometric shape that would show it has been faked or tampered with. These discriminating traits are learned by the proposed model, and it becomes good at recognizing them, hence making it capable of accurately identifying logos.

For training and testing the logo detection models, the input data must be arranged, organized, and made ready by following the below modules. The essential modules involved in the preparation of training testing data are as follows:

LogoDataset Custom: This component is a subclass of `torch.utils.data.Dataset` which is supposed for loading and preparing the logo pictures. As it reads images from a given directory, it also uses folder structure to distinguish between "Fake" and "Genuine" images, and only after then performs image alterations for resizing and normalization.

Image Transformations: A series of pre-processing operations on the logo images is carried out while also includes scaling them to a consistent size (e.g., 224×224 pixels to be compatible with CNN architectures) along with normalizing pixels, and this entire process is called `torchvision.transforms`. By taking these precautions, you can be sure that the model is fed input data in a consistent style that makes training it efficient and effective.

Adaptation for Logo Detection: All these pretrained models' output layers are subject to change to meet the needs of the binary classification task, which is responsible for identifying "Genuine" logos from "Fake" ones. Finally, this adaptation entails fine-tuning the models on the project-specific dataset (in our case for logo detection) and hence deducing the required number of output classes. In our case, it is two output classes, fake and genuine, connected to all hidden layers.

Loss Function: We used CrossEntropyLoss for binary classification problems. We found it is good at handling classification problems.

Optimizer: As model weights are modified depending on training data, we have used the Adam optimizer, which is renowned for its flexible learning rate characteristics. It was selected due to its ability to converge to optimal solutions.

Training Loop: This module is responsible for the iterative process of updating model weights, backpropagation, loss calculation, and batch data feeding into the model. In order to track progress, this loop also uses tools for assessing model performance over epochs.

Finally, the trained models are tested on a different 'test dataset' to evaluate their performance. This module consists of accuracy calculation submodule which is a simplest statistic that provides a quick way to assess the efficacy of the model by figuring out the percentage of correctly detected genuine logos from fake in the test dataset and a model saving module which makes it possible to save learned model weights for later use without requiring retraining. This component is very essential for using the model in practical applications of logo detection or for future study.

4.6 Results and Discussion

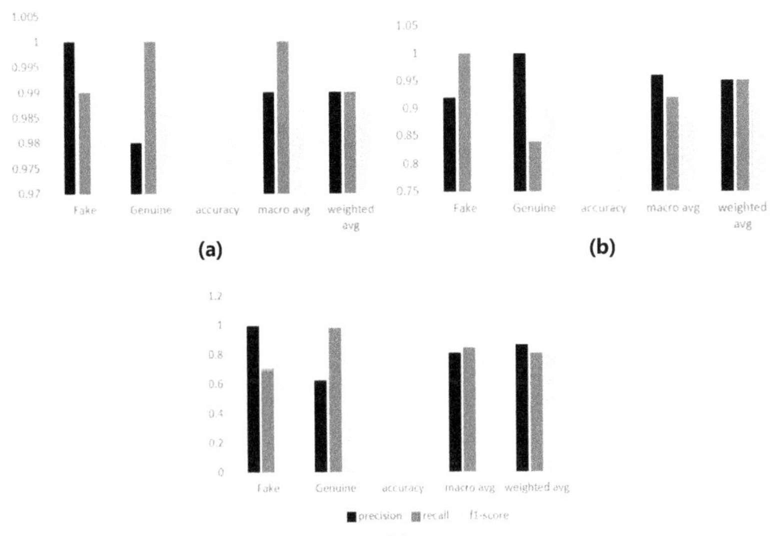

Figure 4.7 Classification metrices of ResNet50(a), EfficientNet(b), InceptionV3(c)

Figure 4.7 (a), (b), and (c) show the results of the precision and recall scores of the three pre-trained DL models for feature extraction. that the model's precision and recall scores are consistently high for fake as well as genuine images, meaning that the model has a good grasp of the data. ResNet50 displays tremendous performance with 99% when it has been compared to the ground truth. F1-scores for both classes (namely fake and guanine) are high, meaning that there is a good trade-off in precision-recall. This implies that ResNet50 is highly efficient in classifying images correctly and therefore can be used reliably for any image classification task.

As seen in Figure 4.7(b), EfficientNet presents the reduced accuracy compared to ResNet50 at 95 percent. It is an excellent network for the detection of fake images with a precision score of 92% but less accurate for genuine images at a recall score of 84%. That is, sometimes genuine images will be misclassified as fake. Still, it shows the efficiency of EfficientNet in handling image classification is acceptable with a relatively smaller computational footprint compared to the larger models.

With inception, 80% of accuracy is attained as visualized in Figure 4.7 (c) with other details. InceptionV3's model is very different from ResNet50 and EfficientNet models. There has been a trade-off in precision and recall, specifically with the detection of true images. The recall score obtained for the true labeled images is high at 98%, whereas the precision is relatively low at 63%. Furthermore, identifying a higher tendency is misleading or misclassifying the genuine images as fake as observed in Figure 4.7(c). Inceptionv3 identifies fake images with a high precision score of 99% while the recall value stays comparatively low at 71%. This signifies that InceptionV3 is not good enough for classifying genuine images correctly with poor delivery in performance.

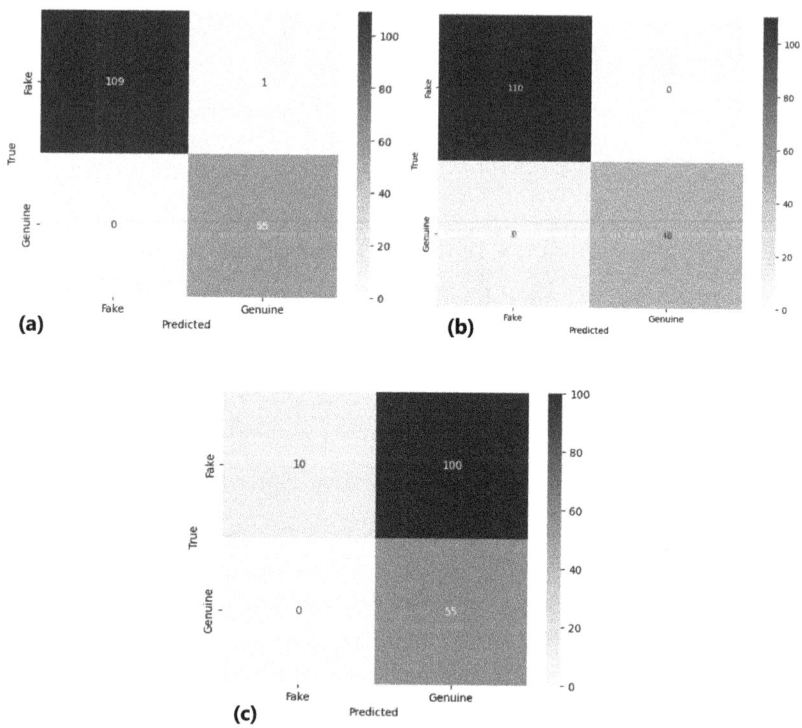

Figure 4.8 Confusion Matrix plotted after model evaluation of ResNet50(d), EfficientNet(e) and InceptionV3(f)

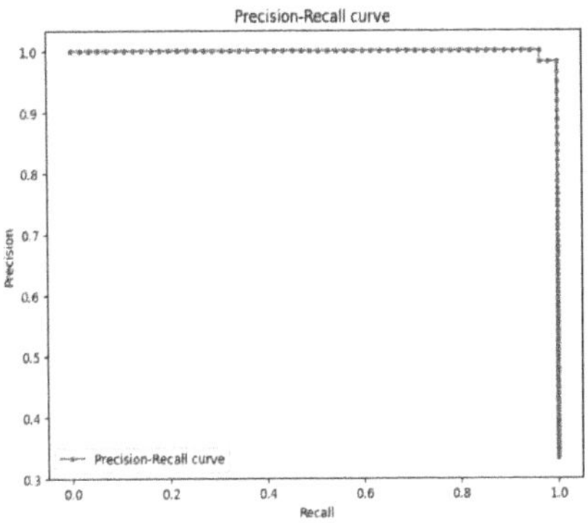

(g)

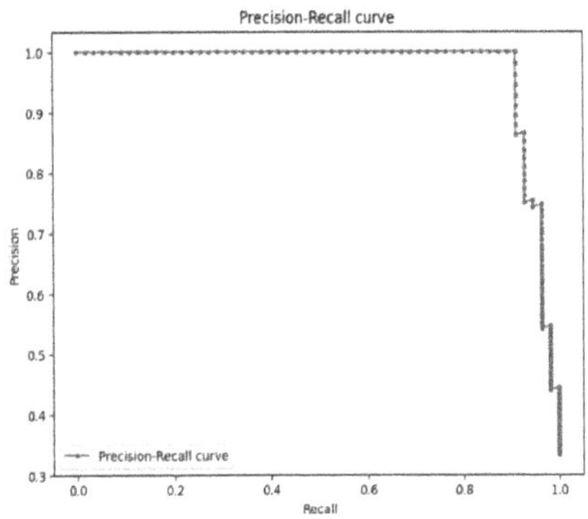

(h)

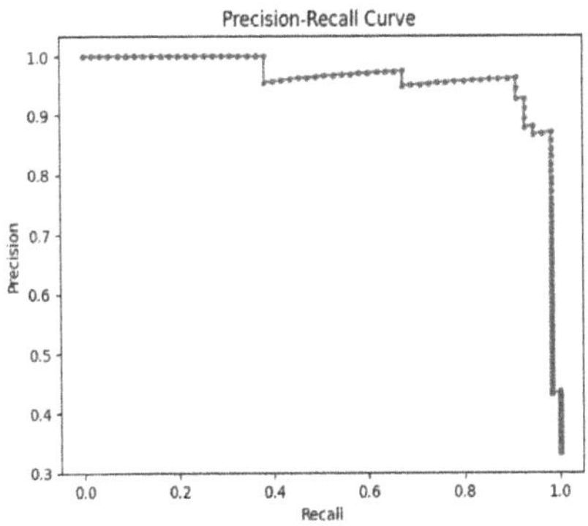

(i)

Figure 4.9 Precision-Recall curve for ResNet50(g), EfficientNet(h), and InceptionV3(i)

Figure 4.8 shows the confusion matrix for test images of the Logo dataset for ResNet50, EfficientNet, and InceptionV3 model. Here, the true labels of the images are used as rows with the predictions given by the model in columns. The diagonal cells count the number of correct classifications for each category and off-diagonal cells reflect the errors in classifications.

This curve is used when there is an important imbalance between the classes to quantify the success of the prediction. One may find the trade-off between recall and precision graphically expressed at different thresholds. High area under the curve is captured by high precision and high recall. A low false positive rate implies high precision, and a low false negative rate implies high recall.

We know,

$$p = \frac{tp}{tp + fp}$$

$$r = \frac{tp}{tp + fn}$$

where p = precision, r = recall, tp = true positives, fp = false positives, fn = false negatives

In Figure 4.9, we can observe the PR curve for implemented algorithms.

A receiver operating characteristic curve is a graphical representation that gives details of a binary class classifier or diagnostic procedure overall operating threshold values. It shows every plausible combination of true positive rate, for short, sensitivity, and false positive rate for different decision

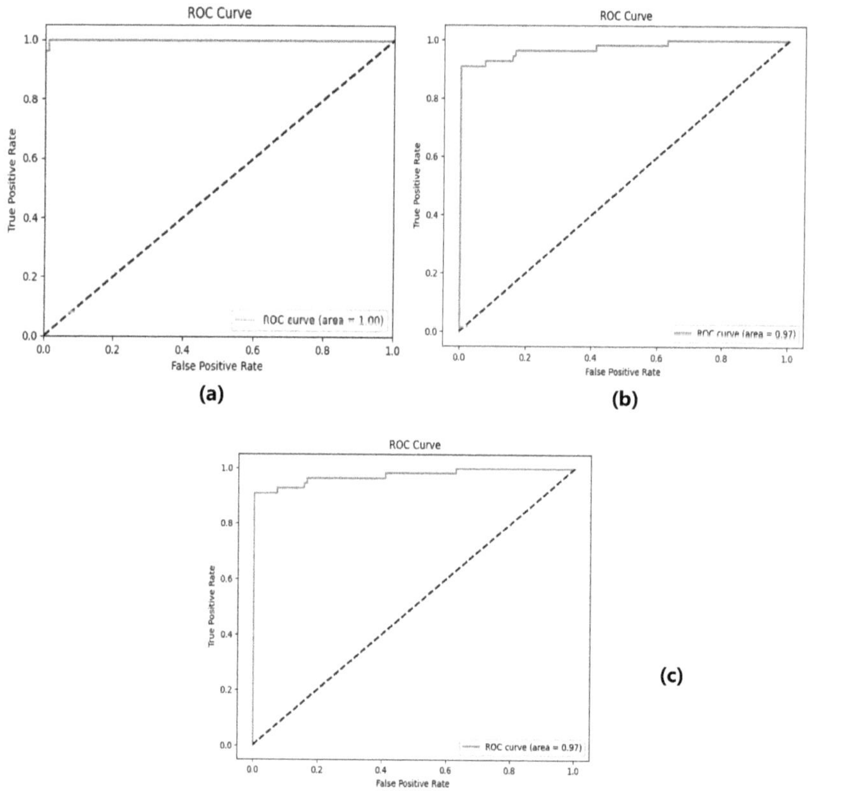

Figure 4.10 Receiver Operating Characteristic (ROC) Curve for ResNet50(j), EfficientNet(k), and InceptionV3(l)

points considering variations. The plot requires two important metrics at the graph plot, namely false positive rate (fpr) and true positive rate (tpr), for sensitivity.

We know,

$$tpr = \frac{tp}{tp + fn}$$

$$fpr = \frac{fp}{fp + tn}$$

where,

tpr = true positive rate, fpr = false positive rate, tp = true positive, tn = true negative, fp = false positive, fn = false negative

In Figure 4.10, the ROC sensitivity can be observed for implemented algorithms.

4.7 Comparison with Existing Works

Table 4.1 Performance metrics of the proposed method

Model	Accuracy	Precision	Recall (Macro Avg.)	Recall (Weighted Avg.)	F1 Score
ResNet50	99%	99%	100%	99%	99%
EfficientNet	95%	95%	92%	95%	94%
InceptionV3	80%	87%	85%	80%	81%

As observed in Table 4.1, there are experimental findings that show the efficacy of our methods in correctly detecting logo-based phishing threats. Traditional spixel-based matching methods were greatly surpassed by refined CNN models achieving a whole 99% accuracy. In practical scenarios, this is very important when the risk of false positives and true negatives is high. Technically, the pre-trained models allowed for fast extraction and classification of features, which reduced computational time compared to building models from scratch. There are many possibilities for practically implementing such models into existing CPS security frameworks with respect to enhancing their ability to detect and prevent phishing attacks.

In fact, our approach demonstrates robustness in handling phishing logos common in different regions, especially South Asia. It has a regional focus that helps it maintain region-specific threats, hence making it more applicable in real-life situations. However, there has been a limitation on if these distorted/ novel logos can be detected efficiently or not as the case may be because of low accuracy rates. As such, future research should aim at developing methods to mitigate these constraints, like expanding the training dataset and refining algorithms, which would improve the generalization capabilities of PHISHDET.

Our approach was based on CNN, and it made use of other models like ResNet50, EfficientNet, and InceptionV3, which were then compared to traditional pixel-based matching techniques, as well as the recent state-of-the-art models used for logo-based phishing detection. Our method significantly improved detection performance compared to a recent study that obtained 87% accuracy from hue values and density distribution obtained from image centroids; the latter only consisted of 21 distinct brand logos. While EfficientNet performed decently with an impressive accuracy of 95%, ResNet50 exceeded the classical hue-based method by a significant margin at 99%. On the other hand, InceptionV3 exhibited high fake image precision but had low overall accuracy at 80 percent. Hence, this demonstrates how our technique is better than other ones that depend on hue alone by offering scalability and real-time CPS security applications that are accurate and robust.

In addition, due to this reliance on what is delivered as input images, the conventional way of doing things suffers from less accuracy and more false positives. In contrast, our CNN-based approach automates feature extraction, hence giving rise to significantly greater precision and robustness. As reported in the literature review, this method achieves an accuracy of 99%, thus outperforming numerous existing methods that obtain typically 85–90% accuracy. On the other hand, other models like EfficientNet and InceptionV3 also performed well, with EfficientNet trading off computational efficiency for accuracy, while InceptionV3 had a high precision but recall rate that was low for true images. To summarize, our approach offers a scalable and efficient solution to logo-based phishing detection in real-time CPS security, surpassing current methodologies on both precision and applicability.

4.8 Conclusion

The challenge of logo-based phishing as a constant and evolving threat is increasing with the continuous proliferation of Cyber-Physical Systems for various online transactional purposes. This paper addressed the challenge by creating an innovative method that aims to detect logo-based phishing threats exclusively for CPS. A comprehensive review of literature indicates several limitations of traditional security solutions and the need for a more sophisticated, adaptive method to counteract logo-based phishing attacks. Based on various studies, we came up with an analysis of pre-trained deep neural networks, figuring out which suits best for the use case, and implemented the neural network with improved accuracy and precision in detecting logo-based phishing attacks.

The main components of the proposed methodology include data acquisition and preprocessing, feature extraction using pretrained convolutional neural networks, fine-tuning of these models, and the creation of custom phishing logo classifiers. Using deep learning with the image processing powers of detecting even the subtlest indicators within logos, our approach will make attempts at detection more efficient by recognizing signs within logos that would point toward manipulated images or fraudulent ones, thereby making them effective cues in mitigating phishes. The working of logos has been tested with various CNN architectures of different types: ResNet50, Inception v3, and EfficientNet, on a wide-ranging dataset covering top firms. Some very encouraging results have been derived from the same. These results highlighted that a diverse dataset can help in the explanation of the working of logos on various types of CNNs. In sum, this study is a major step forward in CPS security and provides an approach that is both strong and scalable towards addressing the rising problem of logo-based phishing attacks. Future work should concentrate on improving and confirming this methodology for assimilating it into present security systems as well as deploying it in practical contexts to combat the escalating danger of logo-based phishing attacks in the online world today.

5 Impact of Cyberattacks

Abstract: Cyber-attacks have far-reaching consequences that extend beyond financial losses, affecting businesses, individuals, and national security. This paper explores the multifaceted impact of cyber-attacks, beginning with their economic consequences, such as financial theft, operational disruptions, and recovery costs. It also examines reputational damage, where breaches erode public trust and brand credibility. Additionally, the study analyses societal and national security implications, including threats to critical infrastructure and data privacy. Lastly, it delves into the psychological effects on victims, highlighting stress, anxiety, and fear caused by cybercrime. Understanding these impacts is crucial for developing comprehensive cybersecurity strategies and resilience measures.

Keywords: Cyber-attack consequences, Economic impact, Reputational risk, National security threats, Psychological effects

5.1 Introduction

Cyberattacks have evolved as serious and complex threats for individuals, organizations, and even countries in the digital world. Such hostile intrusion may have some very long-lasting and severe damage, such as causing enormous financial loss to catastrophic failures in critical infrastructure. Among the gravest concerns about cyberattacks is how they can cripple businesses and some of the crucial services upon which modern society rests. Cybercriminals may strategically target a business's critical infrastructure, such as a power grid, transportation system, or financial institution, with the aim of causing further widespread and cascading damage. The impact of these attacks may then be simply devastating, such as long-term service interruptions, vast financial losses, and even physical harm. For example, if a cyberattack on a power grid is very successful, a widespread blackout could leave essential services crippled and cause vast economic and social disruption. Conversely, a serious cyberattack against a transportation network could severely restrict the movement of goods and persons, leading to supply chain breaks and severe economic consequences [15]. Widespread, cascading impacts of cyberattacks pose a great and escalating risk to the stability, security, and very makeup of modern societies.

5.2 Economic Consequences

Cyberattacks pose an enormous and rising threat to the world economy, causing significant financial losses and disrupting essential services. The financial impact of the attack extends far beyond the immediate costs of reparation, touching businesses, individuals, and even national economies. These cyberattacks can have far-reaching and devastating impacts, and they result in extreme financial losses, extended service disruptions, and, in some cases, widespread physical harm. It covers not only initial incident response and data recovery activities but also various legal and regulatory fees, interruptions of business, reputational damage. These attacks can cause indirect costs of even more sizeable proportions that include lost revenues, increased premiums for insurance policies, and dislocations in the supply chain. At the level of the economy, cyberattacks might disrupt economic activities, slow growth, increase the rate of unemployment, and possibly have national security implications. The economic impact from cyberattacks grows with each new day, posing a significant necessity for proactive measures in comprehensive security.

5.2.1 Direct cost

The direct costs of cyberattacks can be quite high and include a host of expenses an organization has to incur. The impact of these costs can severely affect the financial stability and running of a business.

Incident response: Even the investigation phase, containing damage and regaining systems, would be very cost-intensive. A lot of specialist cybersecurity experts usually have to be hired, involved in deep forensic analysis, with comprehensive remedial measures to remove the vulnerabilities under which the attackers compromised the system [16].

Data recovery: In ransomware attacks, it can be expensive to recover lost or corrupted data and even potential ransom payments. Therefore, the cost of organizations should be reduced through robust data backup and recovery solutions to make the critical information available.

Legal and regulatory fees: Cyberattacks mostly lead to cases in courts, fines by regulators, and the cost of complying. Organizations might have to hire lawyers, settle the cases, and follow the industry's required standards; these costs are likely to be heavy [17].

Business disruption: Cyberattacks will significantly reduce lost productivity and operations disruption and lost revenues and missed deadlines with lowered productivity. It has profound consequences for the bottom line and general competitiveness of the organization.

Reputational damage: Intangible costs associated with reputational damage, loss of customer trust, and reduction in brand value can be highly destructive. An effective cyberattack can undermine the confidence of customers, blemish the reputation of the organization, and cause a considerable loss of market share, thus adding to the financial loss.

5.2.2 Indirect Cost

Lost revenue: Cyberattacks cause huge losses in revenues for organizations that fall prey to such attacks. Such attacks reduce sales, lost contracts, and reduced market share because of the damage done to reputation and service disruptions caused by them. If the company's systems are compromised or operations are disrupted, then it will fail to fulfill its obligations to its customers, leading to orders being cancelled and business opportunities being lost. Moreover, once trust and the brand reputation have been eroded as a result of a successful cyberattack [18], the organization might face difficulties retaining current customers and even attracting new ones, worsening the revenue fall further. This financial loss may prove to be sizeable in its own right and prevent the firm from recovering in time to make adequate investments in securing itself to protect against further attacks.

Higher insurance premiums: The organization's face is far higher premium cybersecurity insurance rates shortly after the incidence of a cyberattack. The insurers are looking for increased risk in the organization due to this exposure and, for sure, any future claims because of such a breach. High-cost premiums further worsen an organizational financial resource issue, shifting many funds from various other key operational and investment issues. The increased financial load from the cyberattack, besides the economic impact, also hinders the ability of the affected organization to recover and employ essential security improvement measures to prevent such events.

Investment in security upgrades: Implementation of new, higher levels of security can be quite expensive in the way of deterring future cyberattacks. Various upgrades have to be invested in by an organization to secure itself by modernizing outmoded software and hardware, putting up sophisticated detection and response capacities for threats, and increasing cybersecurity education among the employees. Investments can be as straightforward as buying new security technologies up to hiring a specific cybersecurity person and robust security protocols and processes. An organization may need to do a high-level risk assessment, ensure all access controls are secure, and maintain robust systems for backup and recovery in the event that the attack is successful and business operations need to resume. Indeed, the costs of security measures can be very high in terms of maintenance, updates, and testing to stand guard against these latest threats. However, it would be a good investment for the critical assets of an organization and maintaining customer trust over time, ensuring that they remain resilient against the ever-growing level of sophisticated cyberattacks [19].

Investment in security upgrades: It requires massive investments into enhanced security upgrades in the aftermath of cyberattacks that can take a significant chunk of time, which will result in financial outlay for improving old software and hardware and the need for better cybersecurity threats and detection measures as well as the advancement in employee education regarding cybersecurity threats. These can be new security technologies purchased, new cybersecurity personnel hired, and solid security protocols and processes put in place. Furthermore, organizations should be required to do thorough risk assessments, ensure proper access controls are implemented, and put in place effective backup and recovery systems that allow for business to continue running should the attack prove successful [20]. This kind of investment can be very costly because it requires constant maintenance, upgrading, and testing to ensure its effectiveness against the changing dynamics of threats. These are, however, critical investments for safeguarding an organization's critical assets, protecting customer confidence, and long-term capacity in this environment to counter the increasing threat of sophisticated cyberattacks.

Economic impact: Advanced cyberattacks that target any organization's third-party providers, such as vendors, partners, or others, can derail its supply chain significantly. Compromise of intermediaries in the supply chain results in delays, inventory shortages, and an inability to fulfill orders to customers in due time. The organization will likely lose revenue, damage customer relationships, and experience a loss in reputation. Besides the cost of finding and fixing supply chain vulnerabilities and potential fines and penalties in terms of legal liability from regulators, these are just additional burdens that make the cost more onerous. Organizations must assess and mitigate risks from the supply chain proactively, put security controls in place within their ecosystem of partners, and maintain contingency plans for business continuity in case a cyberattack successfully breaches the organization's supply chain.

5.2.3 Macroeconomic Impact

Cyberattacks can also have significant macroeconomic consequences:

Reduced economic growth: Widespread cyberattacks can become a highly damaging effect on economic growth because they interfere with various sectors of economic activity. These attacks tend to drive down the productivity and output scale in many industries and sectors. Losses in revenue, customers unable to receive their orders, or contractual obligations not being met are eventual consequences of downtimes when the organization's operations are compromised by such a successful cyberattack. Such a disruption can trickle down into the greater economy. In other words, when one firm's productivity and output are compromised, then the suppliers, partners, and customers of such an affected firm could also be impacted. Besides, recovery from a cyberattack, say by investing in strengthened security measures, entails diverting funds from productive economic activities toward financial costs for regulatory and legal compliance. All of these factors could add up to a general drag on economic growth as the economy battles to get its footing in the aftermath of a significant cybersecurity event.

Increased unemployment: Successful cyberattacks will be devastating, affecting employment, leading to broad business closures, and massive losses in jobs. Once a well-established organization succumbs to cyberattacks, then the operations might be affected or even halted in their tracks because the revenue channels may be intercepted. In these situations, cutting down on people and costs seems like the way to go forward, but lay-offs and shutting down may end up having another kind of destructive impact: laid-off workers looking for new job opportunities after an attack. Loss of income and reduced economic activity will also add to the unemployment crisis because businesses and consumers are going to cut back due to the uncertain environment. The macroeconomic effects of rising joblessness can be quite severe, as they would affect overall economic recovery and cause long-term challenges for people, families, and communities in terms of consequences from major cyberattacks.

Market volatility: Cyberattacks can impact the financial markets enormously, and subsequent volatility and uncertainty can shatter investor confidence. Successful cyberattacks against leading corporate houses, banks, and institutions or infrastructure critical to national stability can make them lose people's trust and will cause a tremendous fluctuation in stock prices, currency values, and market indices. Investors may lose confidence in the risks that cyber threats pose and thus divest from affected sectors or markets, which can exacerbate the instability in the market. This instability can continue long after the initial shock of an attack since the long-term implications and even regulatory changes are not known. This disruption to normal market operations and erosion of investor confidence can have a wide-ranging impact on the overall economic health and stability, thus making the financial system more vulnerable to the ripple effects of major cyberattacks.

National security implication: Critical Infrastructure Cyberattacks on power grids, transportation networks, or water treatment facilities that will threaten to seriously impair the delivery of critical services indispensable to the conduct of society and economy. In fact, a failure or degradation in such crucial systems can unleash widespread chaos effects that could run throughout various other systems and therefore may threaten to imperil safety of the public, national security, and overall welfare of citizens at large [21]. Such implications could run quite far in potential impact on the nation's defenses, emergency operations, and overall ability to uphold public order and stability. Such national security threats must be met with a holistic, multi-layered response that incorporates increased cybersecurity protections, solid contingency planning, and cooperation between the government, the private sector, and the greater security community.

The economic and social consequences of cyberattacks raise, therefore, worries for businesses, governments, and everyday citizens. Its increasing frequency, scale, and intensity leave demands for more aggressive, multi-layered defenses against cyber threats. This should be strong, preventive measures at safeguarding critical systems and data that are useful in containing breaches whose impact has been reduced by effective incident response and recovery plans and continued investment in security awareness training to empower employees as the first line of defense. What's needed for more resilience and a defense against such cascading effects on the economic, social, and national security scales of massive cyber incidents are broad technological, operational, and human aspects. Indeed, such a comprehensive and collaborative approach to cybersecurity is all the more crucial given the escalating need for reliance on digital technologies.

5.3 Reputational Damage

Of all the crucial consequences of a cyberattack, reputation damage constitutes one of the worst and most dire outcomes in a potential loss. It may far outweigh what will be experienced immediately in actual loss of assets used to retrieve an organization to pre-attack positions. It would drastically threaten eroded customer trust, considerable depreciation in value and standing for an organization's brand, with very far-reaching negative impacts on both the overall bottom-line financial performance and long-term sustainability. The customer lost trust in which the organization was unable to reassure him about protection over his sensitive information and concern, leading to a drastic revenue reduction as a result of keeping off their business since the organization cannot guarantee secure protection of sensitive information and concerns. This eventually creeps into the deterioration of the brand and the economic value of the brand in the market, thereby posing a serious challenge to attracting new and retaining old customers. Notably, a lost reputation can also not allow the organization to raise further capital and thus attract investment needed to innovate or expand and also maintain its comparative advantage. Actually, the recovery process of an organisation from reputational damage is a long and resource-intensive process requiring well-coordinated concerted efforts in order to put into place more stringent cybersecurity safeguards, enhance the transparency of operations, and provide credible assurance for a genuine intent to protect consumer data and confidence. The far-reaching and long-lasting consequences of reputational damage following a successful cyberattack may even threaten the existence of the organization, calling for holistic and proactive security and reputation management [22].

5.3.1 Impact of Reputational Damage

The impact on the organization if its reputation becomes damaged due to a cyberattack can be extensive and severe. Sometimes, loss of customer trust tends to be significant, as this can lead people to take away their business when they perceive an organization as either unable or unfit to protect customers' sensitive information. This customer confidence erosion hits the bottom line directly because, first, they lose the base customers and can't attract potential new ones who will come and support it. Apart from this, an organization's repute can lose much of its value if marred by tainted issues. This often makes it a challenge to be competitive in the market. Where the reputation is suffering, this will also pose a challenge on whether the organization would be able to attract new clients or retain old clients, and it will lose part of its share in the market as competitors use the opportunity and take advantage. Reputational damage can further make it difficult for the organization to attract investment and raise capital since investors may be unwilling to trust their money to an entity whose reputation is already damaged. This will further jeopardize the growth and innovation capacity of the organization, thus amplifying the long-term effects of the cyberattack.

Loss of customer trust is especially damaging for an organization in case of a cyberattack. A customer feels cheated and loses faith in the ability of the organization to protect its sensitive information; thus, customers shift their businesses to other places they believe to be more secure. This erosion of trust directly and indirectly can have an effect on the bottom line of the organization, where it is failing to retain the customers it has already acquired and attract new ones. Rebuilding this trust would take a long and arduous process requiring significant investment in upgrading the cybersecurity of the organization, enhancing transparency, and a genuine effort at protecting the customer's information. This can lead to the loss of customer confidence and undermine the market position, brand reputation, and long-term viability of the organization.

Reduced brand value: A damaged brand reputation can diminish the value of the organization's brand significantly, affecting its ability to attract new clients and retain a current client list. As the reputation of the brand is affected negatively, the organization's market share and competitive advantages may be damaged significantly, so that it loses its market to competitors who gain an advantage. It can have serious effects on an organization from losing brand value, affecting the general financial performance of the organization, as well as long-term sustainability in trying to win back customers' trust and rebuild its reputation within the market.

Reduced market share: It further results in an important reduction of an organization's market share by decreased customer trust and a resultant devaluation of a brand. Because competitors will immediately seize this vulnerable position, competitors are going to win away most of these disenchanted customers. Those disappointed customers may turn away because of lost confidence that the organization cannot keep their personal data secure or the organization has a bad reputation concerning its services. In all these ways, this erosion can severely undermine an organization's position within its market, let rival firms develop a stronger stronghold, and therefore increase their relative market share on the back of the compromised one. Furthermore, the weakening of brand reputation makes it even more challenging to attract new customers and impossible to regain lost ground once the decline is established. This can be very vicious. Recovery from such reputational damage and regaining the trust of customers is a hard and resource-consuming process, requiring a unified, long-term effort to raise the bar on cybersecurity measures, be more transparent, and genuinely show that protecting the interests of customers is paramount.

Damage to reputation also affects the inability of an organization to attract new investment and generate the capital that would be necessary for growth and innovation. Investors view the organization as a bad risk, not trusting their money with an entity proven vulnerable to cyberattacks and that cannot protect its sensitive data appropriately. This fear of investing will significantly strangle the financial muscle of an organization, limiting its ability to grow, innovate on new products and services, or obtain a better market position in terms of a competitive advantage. With the inability to access the right capital to facilitate strategic initiatives, the organization runs the risk of getting outrun by the competition in an endless circle of shrinking market share and erosion of brand value. Rebuilding investor confidence after the occurrence of a major cyber event is a cumbersome, time-consuming process that has to be driven by the organization's clear demonstration of strong cybersecurity posture, proper communication, and a commitment towards protecting customer data. Until the trust is built, the prospect of growth would remain severely throttled, with the long-term impact of the initial cyber incident being further accelerated.

Increased regulatory scrutiny is usually the aftermath of a successful cyberattack, as governing bodies attempt to make accountable those organizations that have been compromised, along with ensuring that sensitive data and critical infrastructure are properly protected. This could mean heavy fines imposed on the organizations, for example, huge fines paid due to poor security or failure to observe industry-specific data protection rules. More fundamentally, the regulator may demand strong new compliance regulations that will burden the targeted organization with the expenditure of considerable sums of money and resources in developing new cybersecurity safeguards, robust monitoring and reporting infrastructures, and regular third-party audits. In this way, the heightened regulatory demands may overwhelm an organization's treasury, taking precious funds away from its core operations and innovation drivers and possibly driving it to financial insolvency over the long run. Navigating this heightened level of regulatory environment in the wake of a successful cyberattack can be something both time-consuming and expensive, with further implications for the future, too, on the organizational total performance.

5.4 Societal and National Security Implications

Cyberattacks represent a deep and complex threat that goes beyond individual organizations' threats, reaching to the very core of the well-being and security of societies and nations globally. They have an ominously high capability to breach critical infrastructure, alter information flows, and deeply undermine public confidence—which is why they are now a leading concern for governments and citizens around the world. These cyber threats are pervasive and evolving, requiring a broad and proactive protection strategy safeguarding societal stability, economic prosperity, and national security interests. In the event that these challenges are not adequately addressed, chaos on a wide scale is likely, severe political instability, and democratic institutions decline with far-reaching consequences for the international community.

5.4.1 Societal Implications

The societal impact of cyberattacks can be far-reaching and disruptive:

Disruption of basic services: A cyberattack that targets the power grid, a healthcare system, or a financial institution can cause absolute devastation because the critical infrastructure involved provides essential services that form the foundation of the well-being and economic stability of society. Such basic essentials as electricity, clean water, and medical care can be impacted significantly, severely compromising emergency response capabilities and potentially endangering the public safety of a catastrophic attack. Such losses may have widespread and long-lasting ripple effects upon individuals and communities alike, touching an entire nation because of the essential services it provides. Such an effect of such an attack may, in fact, be cascaded and propagate through several interconnected systems, causing the impact and disruption to pile up as different governments, business houses, and the public respond to such problems. A proper and effective way to address these threats to critical infrastructure is to have a proactive approach that will consider cybersecurity, resilience, and protection of essential services as the core of a working society.

Public trust is another loss caused by cyberattacks; they have a highly destructive and injurious influence on public trust by destroying the credibility and legitimacy of critical institutions, governments, and online platforms. Data breaches, particularly those that release sensitive personal information, can breed massive skepticism and mistrust across the population and foster social unrest, political instability, and social contract breakdown. It damages public trust such that the proper communication, responses, and measures to regain such confidence by organizational and governmental representatives are severely disrupted. Without confidence in the protection and integrity of critical systems and services, citizens' restoration requires much more extensive efforts, entailing a wide ramification for broader societal well-being and democratic establishment stability. Rebuilding such trust requires sustained, transparent, and comprehensive effort in enhancing the measures of cybersecurity, demonstrating accountability, and being able to credibly reassure that public interests and personal data are safe.

Cyberattacks can also be used for mass-scale dissemination of misinformation and propaganda, influencing public opinion and sometimes even causing social unrest or even violence. It can cause chaos and political or social confusion throughout the land when false information is spread through multiple social media and messaging applications with lightning speed on the internet. These tactics may be exploited by actors from nation-state groups to extremist organizations with the purpose of amplifying divisive narratives, delegitimizing sources of authority, and gradually eroding public confidence in institutions as well as democratic norms. They then continue to diffuse their harmful effects long after the cyberattack with the polarization, muzzling critical discourse, and corroding communities' integrity from harmful information. A robust response to this threat is therefore multifaceted and encompasses sound cybersecurity, education on media literacy, and fostering transparency and accountability in the digital environment.

Catastrophic results: A data breach may bring some devastating effects on a person by letting the sensitive information be exposed, which becomes a disastrous impact on his life. Unauthorized access to private data coupled with its exposure may lead to identity theft, financial catastrophe, and even emotional shock which may prove life-threatening for a person's psyche. The affected individuals might realize that rebuilding a credit report may be a Herculean task, especially in regaining their financial comfort and living through the realization of the fact that the whole issue leaves a psychological scarring effect upon them. This interference can greatly affect their whole well-being and cause trouble in both their personal lives and professional lives, as well as expose them to all issues that may rise from such a breach of data. It might become catastrophic if such breaches occur because the damage and disturbance created are usually profound and long-lasting after the event has occurred.

Impact on public health: The aftereffects of cyberattacks on healthcare can be disastrous, such as disruption of important patient care services, delayed detection of life-changing conditions, or even loss of life that otherwise could have been prevented. The significant impacts on the public health because of widespread medical service disruption, theft and exposure of sensitive data of patients and manipulation of potentially life-saving drugs and medical appliances may be heavy. Such attacks could jeopardize timely delivery of emergency care, compromise the integrity of medical records, and disrupt proper working of connected medical equipment-all these factors could put the patients at a direct risk to their health and safety. Such cyberattacks can have some devastating cascading effects on the healthcare sector by weakening the public's trust in the system, degrading the quality of care provided, and even exacerbating prevailing health crises. An integrated proactive approach is necessary to add layers to cybersecurity measures and ensure the resilience of critical medical services to such threats to the healthcare infrastructure.

5.4.2 National Security Implications

Cyberattacks also pose significant national security risks:

Espionage and stealing sensitive information are also uses of sophisticated cyberattacks by a state-sponsored actor to secretly get into secure networks, databases, and communication lines of the government in order to gain unauthorized access to a very wide range of sensitive information; for example, classified military secrets, strategic plans, and technological innovation that undergird national defense capabilities. The loss of such vital intelligence has the potential to seriously compromise the security posture of a nation by putting its people and vital national interests at stake. Furthermore, the theft of important intellectual properties and trade secrets is likely to strip the country's targeted industries of their economic competitiveness. Such blatant cyber espionage can also put pressure on diplomatic relations, which will be tearing apart nations' trust and collaboration with each other and can further fuel an increase in geopolitical tensions. In such cascading effects of state-sponsored cyberattacks, the crises can be very wide-ranging in nature and can pose a threat to national security, economic stability, and international stability itself.

Critical infrastructure sabotage: Sabotage through cyberattacks against such critical infrastructure can be highly damaging, as for example with cyberattacks against a power grid or the transportation and communication networks. Deliberate disruption of such important systems will produce widespread and cascading impacts when these attacks can be used for the intentional act of sabotaging and disrupting essential systems that ensure the continuity of power, transportation, and communications. This can lead to a national emergency as the loss of such valuable services will imperil public safety, hinder emergency response capabilities, and disrupt vital goods and services delivery. The cascading nature of the attacks means that the damage will be further multiplied by the failure in one infrastructure component that prompts failures in other dependent systems, multiple problems culminating in troublesome and exponentially difficult efforts to recover and restore. The sheer scale and severity of potential impacts on national security, public welfare, and economic stability underscore grave threats from the cyberattacks targeting the critical infrastructure.

Election interference: Cyber threats can even threaten to completely undermine democratic elections, leading to a devastating erosion of the foundations upon which democratic governance is structured. By affecting the voter registration database, spewing false information, and bringing down electoral processes, election hijacking could thus be ensured in the shadows of cybercrimes. An all-embracing, multi-pronged approach, which must include not just robust cybersecurity practices but also public awareness on media literacy and how to be promoted in a sense of digital responsibility and transparency, has to be provided. Securing the sacred act of election ensures maintaining the foundation upon which the real essence of democracy is derived with the intent to reflect people's will at best.

Increase in cyberweapons: The building and proliferation of advanced cyber weapons are grave and complicated threats to national security. Advanced digital weapons can be used by all powerful state actors as well as by many non-state groups to launch horrendous attacks upon the critical infrastructure systems of a nation, its military prowess, and key institutions. These cyber weapons are particularly destructive just because of their pervasive spread and ease of access and their relative anonymity and deniability that they also lend. It may be deployed, for example, by adversaries to cripple essential services and to destroy sensitive data as well as even a cascading effect on systems within an interlock. The far-reaching consequences of such attacks have the potential to paralyze a nation, with the ultimate impact being very negative on security, economic stability, and public welfare. An overarching, multilateral approach to meet the challenge of cyberweapon proliferation must include powerful defensive measures along with international cooperation and a rejuvenated focus on cybersecurity resilience. If this changing threat is not addressed, the world's countries may find themselves with an ever greater susceptibility to devastating impact from these dangerous digital weapons.

Escalation of international tensions: Given their potential in cyberattacks for creating high prospects for escalating tensions in international arenas and even armed confrontations, even these operations involving such complexities along with anonymity facilitate misinterpretations that can often contribute to heightened miscalculation. A poorly defined international set of norms and protocols for how to respond to cyberattacks presents a backdoor that the adversary could take advantage of. Such indistinctness could even sharpen the already simmering geopolitics because when the countries perceive this form of aggression, they won't know what to do, hence forcing them to react with all the vigor that is at their disposal. Such interconnectivity poses a danger of causing unintended and uncontrollable escalations since one cyberattack could have far-reaching, unpredictable, and uncontrollable effects on the interconnectivity of critical infrastructure and communication networks throughout the world. The challenge it brings requires developing more robust international agreements, information sharing, and clearly defined guidelines on responsible state behavior in the digital domain. Failure to do so would undermine global stability and raise the risk of catastrophic conflict.

5.5 Psychological Impact on Victims

Beyond the technical and financial impact, cyberattacks can infuse deep psychological stress on individuals and communities. The mental trauma or emotional stress that can be generated as a result of these attacks is overlooked by the material loss and the consequent damages. Developing an understanding of psychological effects and their management is essential to providing proper support and resilience in facing this growing threat. Such factors as privacy violation, lack of control over personal data, and unknown impact of a cyberattack may be strong stimuli to experience extreme fear and anxiety or feelings of being violated. In general, they feel unsafe and become concerned with further attacks or their long-term impact on personal lives. It's extremely stressful, as such factors may provoke extreme feelings of losing control and sense of security. Anger and frustration, for example, are common responses to the obvious injustice of targeting a victim and to the often complex and confusing recovery process. Anger may therefore be expressed towards the perpetrators, the institutions who are seen as having enabled the wrongdoers' access to their victim, or themselves, who may have done everything in their power to avoid the attack.

It may further be associated with the psychological aftermath of the attack, causing a victim to be embarrassed, feel ashamed, or even become reclusive from social circles. People feel shame and embarrassment due to the vulnerability involved in an attack that uses their sensitive personal data or even finances. The resulting depression and withdrawal from society lead to deep-rooted vulnerability even after the resolution of technical and financial facets. Even severe cases of cyberattacks can make the victims suffer from post-traumatic stress disorder, flashbacks, nightmares, and other trauma symptoms. It is especially so in cases involving threats of violence, harassment, or stalking that can leave lasting emotional scars and profoundly affect the sense of safety and well-being of an individual. This means the psychological impact of cyberattacks has to be dealt with to provide support to individuals and communities and make them resilient in case of such incidents. By understanding that these are psychological traumas for victims and providing the necessary mental health care and counseling, we can enable them to better cope with recovery and resilience against these rising threats.

Common responses from victims of cyberattacks are very wide and are on a full spectrum of intensive emotional and psychological responses, thereby having very crucial and long-term impacts on well-being. Some possible reactions could range from fear and anxiety to anger and frustration, shame, embarrassment, depression, and social isolation, among others, but the extreme will be post-traumatic stress disorder symptomatology. Some of these are mentioned below.

Fear and anxiety: The invasion of privacy, lack of control, and uncertainty regarding the extent of the damage done during a cyberattack can be causes of deep-seated and wide-ranging fear and anxiety among the victims. Victims might feel an intense obsessive concern over possible future attacks with a fear that the safety and security of their private information would never be the same again. Such feelings of vulnerability and loss of control can be truly unsettling, as victims are perpetually placed on high alert in expectation of further assault or disruption of their lives.

Anger and frustration: The sense of injustice, helplessness, and the complexity of going through the process of recovery after a cyberattack may cause them to feel strongly angry and frustrated. Victims will then express anger at the perpetrators who violated their security and personal information, or perhaps anger at themselves for being targeted, or anger at the institutions and organizations they blame for their vulnerability. This emotional response will naturally emerge following the cyberattack and resulting traumatic change in status, but there is an equally strong need for these emotions to be met by support mechanisms to enable a proper resolution to these psychological effects in rebuilding a new secure environment with renewed control.

Shame and embarrassment: Sometimes, a person may feel ashamed or embarrassed to be subjected to such attacks, especially where sensitive information belonging to a victim is revealed and financial losses result. Even to the point where they question what they have done wrong since appropriate measures to guard their cyberspace were put into place. These feelings of blame and stigma really debilitate a victim because they not only suffer the traumatic effects psychologically but also emotionally as well. Overcoming these feelings of shame and embarrassment is crucial to empower the victim to move ahead in the process of recovery.

Depression and isolation: The impact of a cyberattack on the human psyche can manifest in depression and social withdrawal-isolation. Often, victims can't cope with this emotional aftermath. They withdraw into themselves, isolate themselves from other people, and cut off themselves from support systems as they cope with the violation and trauma the attack has perpetrated. This self-inflicted isolation would further compound psychological impacts, and it would further make it more difficult for the victims to be able to seek the resources needed to heal and regain some stability in life.

Cyberattacks may bring post-traumatic stress disorder to their victim: Flashbacks, nightmares, and all those rehabilitating traumas are usually witnessed by someone with this severe mental illness. Severe mental consequences would most certainly result if threats of violence were immediately followed, harassment never quit, or stalking extended periods. They might end a life, as that kind of danger often left severe psychological and personal effects. Violation of personal boundaries and constant fear of further harm trigger extreme hypervigilance, hyperarousal, and vulnerability feelings, which may linger even after the immediate situation is over.

6 Conclusion and Recommendations

Abstract: In an era where cyber threats are increasingly sophisticated, understanding their nature and impact is critical for effective mitigation. This chapter concludes by summarizing key findings on cyber-attacks, their types, evolution, and consequences. It provides policy and practice recommendations aimed at strengthening cybersecurity frameworks, enhancing awareness, and improving defensive strategies against cyber threats. Additionally, the study highlights future research directions, emphasizing the need for advanced detection technologies, stronger regulatory measures, and interdisciplinary collaboration. By addressing these areas, this research contributes to the ongoing efforts to create a more secure digital environment.

Keywords: Cybersecurity strategies, Policy recommendations, Risk mitigation, Future research, Cyber defence

6.1 Summary of Key Points

Cyberattacks have become the norm and a persistent threat in all sectors of society. As attacks grow increasingly sophisticated and occur more frequently, there is a great need for heightened cybersecurity measures as well as for a better understanding of the motives and tactics behind cyber adversaries. It makes the attacks more powerful through the interconnection of our world, thus making it important that the vulnerability existing in all these interconnected systems and infrastructure be addressed.

Key takeaways from a closer look into the anatomy and effect of cyberattacks include:

Evolving threat landscape: An evolving threat landscape, methods, and the evolving targets of cyberattacks are part of a perpetual flux, with adversaries constantly concocting newer, more sophisticated tactics to bypass existing security measures. Such an evolving threat demands a vigilant and adaptive approach, ongoing research, innovation, and refinements in security strategies and technologies. Because cyberattacks are a very dynamic domain of threats where perpetrators are finding and developing advanced toolkits constantly, cybersecurity experts will have to act proactively: anticipate new potential threats in collaboration with appropriate technology, organizational, and human factor solutions. To be vigilant is the only chance for protection for organizations as well as individuals.

Asymmetric warfare: Cyber attacks often represent the form of asymmetric warfare because they allow both non-state players and smaller states to challenge mightier, power-holding enemies. The same asymmetry finds its roots within the inherent advantage cybercriminals and rogue state players have in a digital domain. Using advanced hacking techniques, malware, and vulnerabilities in complex digital systems, these adversary forces can attack the center of an opponent's infrastructure and defense system without having to use the traditional military might or material. These dynamic changes the power equation so that weaker parties can project influence and cause significant disruption even against robust adversaries. It's hard for the old-line military and security organizations to contain and repel the more ubiquitous, boundary-less threats from the Internet when cyberspace seems pervasive and boundless. Dealing with this issue of asymmetric cyber warfare necessitates an integrated solution that encompasses augmented technological defenses, intelligence-sharing improvements, and greater international cooperation against the constantly shifting and dynamic landscape of the threats.

Multi-dimensional impacts: Cyberattacks do not have only monetary effects and data leaks. The severity of the effects can lead to reputational harm, damaging the image of the affected party and weakening the people's confidence in that party's potential. The victims may suffer more from the psychosocial aftermath of the event, with victims feeling violated, terrorized, and constantly threatened by the attacker. The impacts can filter down into communities and can erode social cohesion and damage society at large. The multiple impact nature of harm caused by a cyberattack creates the need to take an integrative approach at mitigation and recovery that goes beyond the financial or data-based ones and reaches out to encompass emotional, reputational, and societal consequences as well.

Attribution challenges: Attribution of cyberattacks is often very challenging and therefore can hinder clear accountability and make it difficult to make effective responses. The inherently anonymous and border-less nature of cyberspace provides anonymity to such perpetrators, whose identity and even the location they operate from could be masked from their victims. The use of spoofing techniques, proxy servers, and vulnerability exploitation in the global digital infrastructure also makes them virtually untraceable. Such unattribution also can actually hinder efforts to hold them accountable by rendering the development of appropriate legal and diplomatic consequences impossible and frustrating efforts at targeted countermeasures. More urgently still, the tactics and tools of cybercriminals and state-sponsored actors are evolving almost too quickly to keep up, with the continuously evolving methods that thus negatively affect the dynamic of attribution. It is important to deter future attacks, to ensure justice, and to ensure that appropriate remedial measures can be put in place by addressing these attribution challenges as part of a comprehensive and effective cybersecurity strategy.

Need for collaboration: It therefore calls for effective cooperation among individuals, the private sector, and the government to strengthen cybersecurity. Multistakeholder coordination helps to share great amounts of information, integrate security strategies, and take comprehensive action against growing cyber threats. Through the accumulation of their resources, experience, and insight, these entities can create a more holistic, proactive defense against an evolving threat environment. This type of collaboration will definitely help in creating a standardized protocol with a clear understanding of the defined lines of communication, timely threat sharing, and power given to each organization and user for being attentive and forecasting upcoming threats early enough, anticipating when the crime would be realized, and reacting appropriately in their case. Ultimately, however, it is the combined effort of governments, businesses, and the public that will prove indispensable to strengthening our digital defenses and securing our interconnected world from the pervasive and persistent threat of cyberattacks.

6.2 Recommendation

A proactive and all-inclusive approach is necessary to address these varied digital threats. This can be done through investment in enhanced cybersecurity infrastructure, such as robust systems like firewalls, intrusion detection tools, and encryption technologies. It is also very important to develop proactive threat intelligence capabilities to detect and mitigate the emerging cyber threats before they become a huge problem. International cooperation is vital for sharing information, coordinating responses, and setting norms of responsible behavior in cyberspace. Strong partnership between the public and private sectors is necessary in developing effective strategies and best practices in cybersecurity. Public awareness and education on potential cybersecurity risks and best practices make individuals better able to protect themselves and their information. Strong laws and frameworks to deter perpetrators should be in place to prevent any future attacks. Sustained investment in cybersecurity research and development is very important to lead the evolving threat and develop more innovative security solutions.

Complementing the technological and strategic measures, it is also a necessity to have incident response preparedness to limit the impact of successful cyberattacks. Clear incident response plans in place ensure speedy and effective recovery, limiting damage and disruption to these incidents. These plans would include procedures on how to identify, contain, and eradicate threats as well as strategies for recovering systems and data. These plans need to be regularly tested and updated in order to effectively face changing attack vectors. In doing so, by having a proactive measure together with the most robust incident response capabilities, we can enhance our defenses, reduce risks, and build a better and more secure future against such "unseen wars."

6.3 Future Research Direction

Future research in the field of cybersecurity has to take into consideration the ever-increasing prowess of the "unseen war" and sophistication in cyberattacks. One of the critical research directions is the intersection of artificial intelligence and cybersecurity. As AI is increasingly being used, the focus of the research should be made on how AI can be best utilized for enhancing threat detection and response capabilities, as well as how risks associated with AI-powered attacks may be mitigated. The other important area of research is in the increasing interconnectedness of devices through the Internet of Things. Securing IoT devices and networks will require new approaches that will deal with the specific challenges these devices pose because of their different functionalities and low processing power. The research into quantum-resistant cryptography would be essential as well, with a view toward preparing for any potential impact on current encryption methods from quantum computing. It is also important to research the security implications of emerging technologies, such as augmented and virtual reality, to predict future threats and vulnerabilities.

Besides technological improvement, human aspects on cybersecurity issues shall also become critical research topics for future research directions. Psychological and behavioral knowledge from studying cyberattacks helps design a sound training awareness mechanism. Identifying motivations and methods applied by adversaries also provides researchers insights into a possible proactive way in developing defense approaches. On one hand, lawfulness and ethical practice dimensions can influence norms and create a level playing field between citizens in developing principles of appropriate use of the system. Research on the economic and social implications of cyberattacks will also guide policymakers in how to develop appropriate measures to address the more comprehensive consequences of these "unseen wars." Through these two paths, we will be able to better prepare for the future of cybersecurity and create a more resilient digital world.

References

[1] Panda P, Mishra AK, Puthal D. A Novel Logo Identification Technique for Logo-Based Phishing Detection in Cyber-Physical Systems. Future Internet. 2022; 14(8):241.

[2] Gaurav Varshney, Manoj Misra, and Pradeep K Atrey. A survey and classification of web phishing detection schemes. Security and Communication Networks, 9(18):6266–6284, 2016.

[3] Alekha Kumar Mishra, Asis Kumar Tripathy, Sowmya Saraswathi, and Meenakshi Das. Prevention of phishing attack in internet-of-things based cyber-physical human system. In High Performance Vision Intelligence, pages 15–32. Springer, 2020.

[4] Meenakshi Das, Sowmya Saraswathi, Rashmi Panda, Alekha Kumar Mishra, and Asis Kumar Tripathy. Exquisite analysis of popular machine learning–based phishing detection techniques for cyber systems. Journal of Applied Security Research, 16(4):538–562, 2021.

[5] Kang Leng Chiew, Ee Hung Chang, Wei King Tiong, et al. Utilisation of website logo for phishing detection. Computers & Security, 54:16–26, 2015.

[6] Ahmet Selman Bozkir and Murat Aydos. Logosense: A companion hog based logo detection scheme for phishing web page and e-mail brand recognition. Computers & Security, 95:101855, 2020.

[7] Wenbin Yao, Yuanhao Ding, and Xiaoyong Li. Deep learning for phishing detec- tion. In 2018 IEEE Intl Conf on Parallel & Distributed Processing with Appli- cations, Ubiquitous Computing & Communications, Big Data & Cloud Comput- ing, Social Computing & Networking, Sustainable Computing & Communications (ISPA/IUCC/BDCloud/SocialCom/ SustainCom), pages 645–650. IEEE, 2018.

[8] Yun Lin, Ruofan Liu, Dinil Mon Divakaran, Jun Yang Ng, Qing Zhou Chan, Yiwen Lu, Yuxuan Si, Fan Zhang, and Jin Song Dong. Phishpedia: A hybrid deep learning based approach to visually identify phishing webpages. In 30th USENIX Security Symposium (USENIX Security 21), pages 3793–3810, 2021.

[9] Ge Wang, He Liu, Sebastian Becerra, Kai Wang, Serge J Belongie, Hovav Shacham, and Stefan Savage. Verilogo: Proactive phishing detection via

logo recognition. Department of Computer Science and Engineering, University of California . . . , 2011.

[10] Routhu Srinivasa Rao and Alwyn Roshan Pais. Jail-phish: An improved search engine based phishing detection system. Computers & Security, 83:246–267, 2019.

[11] Tianrui Peng, Ian Harris, and Yuki Sawa. Detecting phishing attacks using nat- ural language processing and machine learning. In 2018 IEEE 12th international conference on semantic computing (icsc), pages 300–301. IEEE, 2018.

[12] Nureni Ayofe Azeez, Sanjay Misra, Ihotu Agbo Margaret, Luis Fernandez-Sanz, et al. Adopting automated whitelist approach for detecting phishing attacks. Computers & Security, 108:102328, 2021.

[13] Abdul Basit, Maham Zafar, Abdul Rehman Javed, and Zunera Jalil. A novel ensemble machine learning method to detect phishing attack. In 2020 IEEE 23rd International Multitopic Conference (INMIC), pages 1–5. IEEE, 2020.

[14] Ruofan Liu, Yun Lin, Xianglin Yang, Siang Hwee Ng, Dinil Mon Divakaran, and Jin Song Dong. Inferring phishing intention via webpage appearance and dynamics: A deep vision based approach. In 30th {USENIX} Security Symposium ({USENIX} Security 21), 20

[15] Li, Yuchong, and Qinghui Liu. "A comprehensive review study of cyber-attacks and cyber security; Emerging trends and recent developments." Energy Reports 7 (2021): 8176-8186.

[16] Duo, Wenli, MengChu Zhou, and Abdullah Abusorrah. "A survey of cyber attacks on cyber physical systems: Recent advances and challenges." IEEE/CAA Journal of Automatica Sinica 9.5 (2022): 784-800.

[17] Bendovschi, Andreea. "Cyber-attacks–trends, patterns and security countermeasures." Procedia Economics and Finance 28 (2015): 24-31.

[18] Rid, Thomas, and Ben Buchanan. "Attributing cyber attacks." Journal of strategic studies 38.1-2 (2015): 4-37.

[19] Al-Mohannadi, Hamad, et al. "Cyber-attack modeling analysis techniques: An overview." 2016 IEEE 4th international conference on future internet of things and cloud workshops (FiCloudW). IEEE, 2016.

[20] Yamin, Muhammad Mudassar, et al. "Weaponized AI for cyber attacks." Journal of Information Security and Applications 57 (2021): 102722.

[21] Cohen, Fred. "Simulating cyber attacks, defences, and consequences." Computers & Security 18.6 (1999): 479-518.

[22] Gandhi, Robin, et al. "Dimensions of cyber-attacks: Cultural, social, economic, and political." IEEE Technology and Society Magazine 30.1 (2011): 28-38.

www.ingramcontent.com/pod-product-compliance
Ingram Content Group UK Ltd.
Pitfield, Milton Keynes, MK11 3LW, UK
UKHW021342190726
13845UKWH00027B/685